Sahar and **Bobby Hashemi** are the sister and brother team who built Coffee Republic, the UK's original high street coffee chain. Giving up highly paid professional jobs, she a lawyer in London and he an investment banker in New York, they staked everything on a dream – to create the best coffee chain in Britain. Eight years later they are two of our most successful and high-profile entrepreneurs.

Thinking about starting the business of your dreams?

So what's holding you back? Is it the fear of the unknown? If you are even contemplating starting a business of your own, perhaps you feel 'stuck' where you are now? But even being 'stuck' can seem better than facing that fear. That fear of the unknown, of leaving that comfort zone. Entrepreneurship is like an uncharted ocean. But ask yourself this question: Do you have the will and determination to leave dry land and navigate the choppy and sometimes daunting waters that lie before you?

If so, then *Anyone Can Do It* can help you tackle some of those fears, to answer some of the elusive questions about what an entrepreneur must face when making the decision to go for (what can sometimes seem like) that unattainable dream. Authors Sahar and Bobby Hashemi are the dynamic brother and sister team who started one of the most recognizable and high-profile brands in the United Kingdom today – Coffee Republic.

Sahar and Bobby had to leave their comfort zones too, leaving secure jobs to take the plunge. But this is not a business memoir nor mere corporate history. This is a personal story about two ordinary people who 'did it', and who got it right. *Anyone Can Do It* is an inspirational book that chronicles the start and evolution of a genuine success story. Sahar and Bobby take you through their first conversations (when the seed of the idea was planted), to writing the business plan, finding a name, raising money, opening the first store, taking the company public and to the present day when Coffee Republic turns over millions, employs thousands of individuals and has over 100 outlets around the United Kingdom.

Anyone Can Do It offers a myriad of lessons for aspiring entrepreneurs and blows apart the myth that only 'special' people start successful businesses. It's written in an informal style and packed with tips, advice and quotes. Throughout the text are copies of original business plans, early brainstorms and the cruel and duly ignored bank rejection letters.

Sahar and Bobby take the reader step by step through every aspect of starting a business. The process for them wasn't always easy but one thing is for sure, it was the most rewarding journey either of them has taken.

A COF

SAHAR AND BOBBY HASHEMI

ANYONE CAN DO IT

COFFEE REPUBLIC

COFFEE REPUBLIC

OFFEE REPUBLIC

COFFEE REPUBLI

BUILDING COFFEE REPUBLIC FROM OUR KITCHEN TABLE

57 REAL-LIFE LAWS ON ENTREPRENEURSHIP

CAPSTONE

*'Whenever you are asked if you can do a job, tell them
"Certainly I can".
Then get busy and find out how to do it.'*

- THEODORE ROOSEVELT

You see things and say, 'Why?'

But I dream things that never were; and I say 'Why not?'

- GEORGE BERNARD SHAW

This book is dedicated to

The memory of our father
who taught us the value of hard work and commitment

Our mother
who taught us how to dream

Everyone who has ever worked for Coffee Republic:
It is you who have made this dream come true

Other Wiley Editorial Offices

John Wiley & Sons Inc., 111 River Street, Hoboken, NJ 07030, USA

Jossey-Bass, 989 Market Street, San Francisco, CA 94103-1741, USA

Wiley-VCH Verlag GmbH, Boschstr. 12, D-69469 Weinheim, Germany

John Wiley & Sons Australia Ltd, 42 McDougall Street, Milton, Queensland 4064, Australia

John Wiley & Sons (Asia) Pte Ltd, 2 Clementi Loop #02-01, Jin Xing Distripark, Singapore 129809

John Wiley & Sons Canada Ltd, 22 Worcester Road, Etobicoke, Ontario, Canada M9W 1L1

Wiley also publishes its books in a variety of electronic formats. Some content that appears in print may not be available in electronic books.

A catalogue record for this book is available from the British Library and the Library of Congress.

ISBN: 978-1-841-12765-1 (PB)

Typeset by Cylinder
Printed and bound in Great Britain by TJ International Ltd, Padstow, Cornwall

This book is printed on acid-free paper responsibly manufactured from sustainable forestry in which at least two trees are planted for each one used for paper production.

Acknowledgements

We have decided to write this book because we believe that we have a story to tell and that in relating what we did and the things that happened to us as a result, the reader will gain an insight into the journey of entrepreneurship. For anyone aspiring to take that plunge themselves, this book may prove useful because it's a real life case study.

We have approached our writing journey in the same way that we set out on the road to entrepreneurship. We had no idea how to tell our story when we started...we just knew what we wanted to achieve. The rest we thought we could figure out along the way.

In the process of bringing this book to life, we were struck by the similarity between the process of writing and publishing and the process of entrepreneurship itself. It starts from the "light bulb" – that moment when you know you want to write a book. Then you research your book idea to find whether there is a demand for the book in the market (market research), and then write it all in a book proposal (your business plan). Somewhere along the line you get the 'aha!' moment of finding a title. Then you go searching for a publisher (raising finance), and once you've done that you start writing the book (implementation). Then you have to sell and promote the end result. It's the same process and the same tools that we deployed to start Coffee Republic. And it had the same euphoric highs and heartbreaking lows.

Just as it's the case with the journey of entrepreneurship, you're immeasurably helped by the breaks you get from people you encounter along the way and it is those people that we want to thank here:

Friso van Oranje for coming up with the title *Anyone Can Do It* on a cold January morning in Coffee Republic on Fleet street: a title which has shaped the meaning and being of this book.

Mark Allin at Capstone for telling Sahar on an equally grey January afternoon in Coffee Republic in Chiswick: "I really want to publish your book: tell me what will it take for you to let me do it."

Keith Brody, our editor, for taking the sometimes anarchic and always perfectionist whims and demands of an entrepreneur (to whom writing doesn't come easily) with good humour and understanding.

Grace O'Byrne at Capstone for putting it altogether and turning manuscripts, jottings and visualisations into a real tangible book.

Finally, a big thank you to the combined team effort at Capstone and John Wiley: especially Katherine Hieronymus, Julia Lampam, Oriana Di Mascio, Iain Campbell and Adrian Weston. Any creative endeavour that eventually takes root in reality is the result of teamwork and this book would have never materialised without your efforts.

And finally we keep getting asked about whether or not we had any mentors during the growth of Coffee Republic. Thinking about it now, we did: our mentors were our non-executive directors: Nitin Shah, Stephen Thomas and Nicholas Jeffrey. Thank you for giving us support all the way.

Why the Prince's Trust?

We have called this book *Anyone Can Do It* and that title ref lects our upbringing – we were brought up to believe in ourselves and to trust in our own judgement. That our parents gave us this confidence and self-belief is the greatest gift there is. There are so many young people who, sadly, have not been given the same trust they need in themselves in order to fulfil their dreams.

This is where the Prince's Trust comes in. By removing some of the burdens and barriers that are placed in the way of these young people, it enables them to use their own inherent skills and talents to the best effect. The Princes Trust helps them towards to a future in which there is freedom of choice and the possibility to reach one's goals.

The Prince's Trust is thus a physical manifestation of the "anyone can do it" ethic.

It was only recently that the similarity of the Trust's motto 'yes you can' and the title of our book brought to our attention the invaluable role Prince's Trust plays in enabling 14-30 year olds who face barriers to turn their untapped potential into real success. Their Business Start-up Programme offers low interest loans, mentoring and other support.

The staggering fact is that nearly 60% of their start-ups are still trading in their 3rd year - that's DOUBLE the national average! So far they've helped 50,000 young people to launch over 45,000 businesses. That is, on average, one business every half-hour of every working day.

We had no idea about the sort of businesses the Prince's Trust supported until we got the idea to use one of them to do the photography for our book cover. We were truly astonished by the talent we found.

We chose to work with Stuart Hollis, who is an incredible success story. He was unemployed with a wife and baby and nothing more than a dream to start making money from his passion for photography. The Princes Trust helped him with a low interest loan of £3,000, a £200 marketing grant, and matched him with a business mentor, a retired accountant who proved invaluable in teaching him about all the things he didn't know about business. To cut a long story short, Stuart has just photographed Tony Blair and the BBC now regularly commissions him.

There are so many other success stories like Stuart's. The top 50 Trust supported businesses turn over almost £148 million and employ around 2,255. In short the Princes Trust removes the barriers and allows young people to 'activate' the entrepreneurial qualities that everyone has within them.

November 2002
London

Here is just a small selection of press cuttings for *Anyone Can Do It* which we are proud of and some letters from readers which really touched our hearts:

"Budding entrepreneurs will be fascinated, and pick up valuable practical advice along the way."
- MAIL ON SUNDAY

"If you want to start your own business, this is the book you need. It's full of useful information, including the original Coffee Republic business plan. And if you don't want to start your own business, it's a good read anyway."
- BUSINESS LIFE

"If you are thinking of starting your own business, read this book…
a fascinating read."
- EDGE

"…it will interest anyone who has a 'great idea'. If you're not interested in running a business it will still provide a fascinating account of a success story."
- EVENING STANDARD

"Unlike the Nike and Amazon stories, it is not just the account of what happened: it is also part textbook. So on the one hand you get a warts-and-all recounting of events as they happened...but on the other you get practical advice on the things you need to do, and the things you shouldn't, if you're setting up your own business...Essential reading for any budding Richard Branson's."

- **MANAGEMENT TODAY**

"Much of the information is common sense. However, it provides an up-lifting pep talk to all those would-be Hashemi's, sitting on their hands because they lack self-confidence or an idea of where to begin."

- **BUSINESS AM**

"For any self employed aspirant who has been motivated to 'just do it' by the Nike story...or been seduced by Richard Branson's autobiography Losing my Virginity, [or] had their ethical consciousness raised by Anita Roddick's Business as Unusual...this book should push all the right buttons."

- **BUSINESS EYE**

"...you'll love this hands on tell-it-like-it-really-is story. Fun, accessible and really useful."

- **PARIS WOMEN'S NETWORK**

*"**Anyone Can Do It** is an excellent text to support a course on new venture creation. The discussion of what is involved in going from opportunity identification to the launch of the business - which is often ignored in academic textbooks - is a particular strength of the book. It should be recommend reading for all students taking entrepreneurship courses."*

- **PROFESSOR COLIN MASON, HUNTER CENTRE FOR ENTREPRENEURSHIP, UNIVERSITY OF STRATHCLYDE, GLASGOW.**

Dear Sahar and Bobby,

I have been meaning to write to you for sometime to say how much I enjoyed your book and to let you know how much it helped me in setting up my own firm.

I am a solicitor specialising in Town and Country Planning law. Large partnerships did not suit and last December I decided I was going to branch out on my own. I picked up a copy of your book and read it in one evening. I used the business plan model as the basis of my own plan. I opened for business on the 1st May and am enjoying myself enormously.

Your story really did make a difference to me - it was genuine, enthusiastic and gave me the encouragement I need to take a step I have long wanted to.

- RICHARD MAX, RICHARD MAX & CO SOLICITORS

*We are absolutely delighted that you have given us royalties from **Anyone Can Do It**. This money will enable us to help more young people to overcome their barriers and get their lives working and we are extremely grateful.*

- PRINCES TRUST

I am writing to you how much I enjoyed your book. Anybody who is interested will learn a great deal and one thing that really fascinated me is that I suddenly realised that you would both make marvellous film producers! Every piece of advice you give applies to me when I was producing. The first thing to do when making films is to put together a business plan- but it is not called that in the film industry. It is known as a Schedule & Budget! Anybody who wishes to approach a financier to back an idea he has for a film has to have this document and everything happens exactly as you set out in your book. I always thought of ourselves as 'entrepreneurs' when we were making our films and now your book has confirmed that this in fact is exactly what we were.

- LORD BRABOURNE, PRODUCER OF PASSAGE TO INDIA AND MURDER ON THE ORIENT EXPRESS

Just a quick note to say how much I enjoyed your recent book. I read just about every business book I can get my hands on but really felt it was something special. It's only the second time I have written to authors telling them how much I enjoyed their book.

I love the honesty within your book and the obvious passion you have for the company. I'm going to recommend it to all my friends that are right on the verge of starting their first companies but just need that final push! You've inspired a whole new generation of entrepreneurs.

- MICHAEL ACTON SMITH, CEO OF FIREBOX.COM

I initially read the book at the beginning of my business when going through a difficult patch and deciding whether to carry on with my vision and dream. Your story and honest details of your own personal ups & downs was not only something I could relate to but also an enormous inspiration.

As I am launching a designer fashion brand, I too suffer from supplier difficulties and your book reminds me that there is a reason for doing what I'm doing and there is a light at the end of the tunnel on those difficult, lonely days inevitable in setting up a business

I refer to the book frequently and it has become my business bible.

- ELAINE AITKEN, FOUNDER, ME-O-MI LTD BUSINESS

PREFACE

Does the following picture sound familiar to you?

You've always had a couple of great business ideas nestling comfortably somewhere in the back of your mind. You've even secretly entertained taking the plunge and finding out if you could turn these ideas into reality. You really believe that you've come up with a concept that could work and, moreover, you're convinced that you are the right person to bring it to life.

Not only do you have this specific idea for a business that you just know will be successful, you've also always dreamed of one day doing your own thing, of being your own boss. You yearn for the freedom, the independence, the thrill and the satisfaction of bringing your vision to life, with all the rewards that doing so would give you. *Yet you're not doing anything about it!* You keep postponing the pursuit of your dream to some uncertain date in the distant future. Until then the dream remains something you promise yourself you'll follow up one day, so it becomes your light at the end of the tunnel, a great future you can dream about for now, something to keep you going through the daily grind of working life.

> **ASK YOURSELF THIS QUESTION:**
> **WHY AREN'T YOU PURSUING YOUR DREAM NOW?**

Is it because you're in your comfort zone and entrepreneurship is a leap into the unknown? Even though you admit to yourself that this is hardly an exciting or inspiring place to stay, it is still the safe, solid shore with which you're most familiar whilst entrepreneurship is an uncharted ocean, a deep blue sea to fear. The question you really face is this: Do you have the will and determination to leave dry land behind and commit to navigating the choppy and unknown waters of entrepreneurship when you're not even 100% certain that your idea will work? One look at the ocean ahead and perhaps the uncertainties, the unanswered questions, what you think is your lack of expertise and the general fear of the unknown are enough to convince you to sit still in your comfort zone and not move forward. You have no idea what it might be like if you decided to go ahead.

Anyone Can Do It is our answer to the elusive questions about what an entrepreneur faces when he or she is making the decision about whether or not to go ahead in pursuit of their dream. If you want to know what it will be like, then we hope to provide the answers.

We know what it will be like because we've sat in the same comfort zone you're sitting in now and asked ourselves the same questions you'll face if you decide to take the plunge. A few years ago we were just like you, two people with secure jobs but with a dream of something better in the back of our minds that just wouldn't go away. We went for it, and we've lived to tell the tale in the pages that follow.

We are not business school lecturers and thus we are not about to give you a dry, academic story. We are not pretending this is the definitive textbook about how to launch a new business, either. Nor is this a typical business memoir or a corporate history charting the life of the company we founded, Coffee Republic.

This is our personal story. To some extent it is a mix of all of the above, but it is also simply the human story of two aspiring entrepreneurs who followed their business dream. We are two people who in many ways are probably just like you. But two people who stopped 'thinking about it' and actually dipped their toes in the water, achieved their goals, and learned a lot along the way.

We'll tell you what it was like for us to leave the comfort of cushy jobs - jobs for which we had trained for most of our lives - in order to leap into an unknown world of coffee and retailing, things with which we were completely unfamiliar.

The journey we've made has been the most exciting and fulfilling adventure we could ever have dreamed of but it was more than a business adventure. Rather, it was a life journey.

Our story gives you a step-by-step guide to the challenges and difficulties, breakthroughs and breakdowns, joys and frustrations of starting a business. We'll explain what we did and how we did it and perhaps in so doing we will give you the inspiration and some of the knowledge to believe that you can do it, too. We won't gloss over the difficulties and we won't promise you an easy ride, but we will guarantee you that the path we took is the most rewarding road we've ever taken, and even though it's still work, it will turn out to be the most fun you've ever had in your life if you decide to follow it too.

"Life is either a daring adventure or nothing." - NAPOLEON

By taking you through our thought processes, our inspirations, and even our midnight jottings and ramblings you will see the agony and the ecstasy of the entrepreneurial journey in 'living colour'. Then, if you are at the fork in the road where you have to decide whether to pursue your dream or stay in your comfort zone, you can answer this question and decide for yourself:
Why aren't you pursuing your dream?

THE STEPS IN BRIEF

You are about to follow a journey that starts with an idea and ends up in the reality of a public listed company. Within the course of that journey lie a number of key steps, and it is around these that we have mapped out our voyage and built this book.

We believe there is a 'process' to entrepreneurship. A step-by-step methodology that anyone can follow. Very broadly, it involves the following steps.

Step 1 – Are you ready to be an entrepreneur?

We will convince you that anyone can be an entrepreneur.
We will demystify the myth that entrepreneurs are superhuman (they're most definitely not). Then you will be able to make a conscious decision about whether or not entrepreneurship is for you.

Step 2 – Do you have a BIG idea?

If you want the entrepreneurial life, then what business are you going to start? How do you get that 'light bulb' turned on in your head? Or if you already have that great idea that just won't leave you alone at night, how do you know if it's worth pursuing?

Steps 3-7 – The process of turning your idea to a business

Once you've decided that starting out on your own is for you and you've got a basic idea in your grasp, what's next?

- **Step 3** is the first step you actually take with your idea: market research.

- **Step 4** is writing the business plan.

- **Step 5** is raising money.

- **Step 6** is implementing your idea, turning it into an actual business.

- **Step 7** Build it and they will come? This step is about actually running the business you have created.

Step 8 – To grow or not to grow? Once you've implemented your idea, what next? The key isn't just bringing the dream to life. It's about creating a living business and managing the inevitable questions about growth that follow.

We are often asked how long it took us to bring Coffee Republic through this journey. The answer is that it took us almost one year to the day.

The breakdown of our timing was approximately as follows:

Find an idea:	one night and one day
Research the idea:	two months
Write the business plan and raise money:	three months
Find site and implementation; shop fitting and store opening:	seven months
Growth 1-7 locations:	2 years
Growth 7-25 locations:	1 year
Growth 25-75 locations:	2 years

CHAPTER ONE:

CAN ANYONE BE AN ENTREPRENEUR?

TO BE OR NOT TO BE AN ENTREPRENEUR?

DATE: 2 NOVEMBER 1994
LOCATION: A DARK WINTER EVENING
IN A THAI RESTAURANT OFF THE KING'S ROAD, LONDON

SAHAR: *"I really miss the skinny cappuccinos and fat-free muffins from those New York espresso bars. They were so great. I can't believe there is nothing like them in London."*

BOBBY: *"You know, that is a great business idea. When I was at Lehman a colleague of mine put the prospectus of a US chain of coffee bars on my desk. There could be a real opportunity for them in London. Why don't we start one ourselves?"*

SAHAR: *"Because I'm a lawyer! I didn't say I wanted to start selling coffee, I just wanted it as a customer! I'm not a business person."*

BOBBY: *"Trust me, this a great business idea. Lets do it."*

SAHAR: *"You're starting to get on my nerves. I haven't studied hard all my life to chuck in the law and open a coffee bar. Get another of your business school friends to open one with you. You can rely on me as a customer every day, twice a day."*

Sahar never saw herself as an entrepreneur. In fact, it wouldn't be an exaggeration to say that the thought of starting her own business had never even crossed her mind. The need she felt as a customer for a coffee concept turned her into something she never imagined she'd be: an entrepreneur. Bobby, on the other hand, knew a lot about business and how to go about the steps involved in starting one. He lacked the single most important ingredient needed to become an entrepreneur: the great idea.

Both of us, then, arrived at entrepreneurship from quite different starting points. Sahar as a customer, Bobby with a burning desire to simply start his own business.

There is no one, straightforward path that all entrepreneurs have followed. You can stumble upon the path of entrepreneurship in different ways. It can start with a combination of:

- A BIG idea that just won't go away.
- A gap in the market you've spotted as a customer (Sahar's case).
- The deep desire to be captain of your own soul, master of your ship. (You've had enough of corporate politics.)
- An adversity (e.g. losing your job) may spur you on.
- An unexpected event can force you to almost accidentally stumble on a great business opportunity.
- Or just plain boredom with your status quo.

Whatever your motives, we believe a lot of people think it's not an option because they are led to believe that not just anybody can be an entrepreneur and that entrepreneurship is reserved only for superhuman visionaries. We want to prove to you that entrepreneurship is an option open to anybody. It's not born, it's bred. We all have the mettle within us if only we knew how to activate it.

Law 1: Forget about the swashbuckling 'Richard Branson' type

A flick through any number of newspaper articles will be enough to give you the impression that everyone who starts a business is blessed with some sort of genius but we believe that this is a myth, and we desperately want to dispel it.

Legend and conventional wisdom has made us believe that unless you are a swashbuckling extrovert who has loved business since kindergarten (preferably making your first million selling sweets in the playground) and are somehow blessed with otherworldly skills, then starting up on your own is not an option for you. "Unless you've possessed amazing leadership qualities throughout your life then forget about entrepreneurship" is what people say. Worst of all, if you haven't dropped out of school but are instead well educated and have had a conventional and moderately successful time on the career ladder then you can definitely cross out entrepreneurship as an option for your future.

Rubbish. The truth is that conventional wisdom should be discarded! It's just not accurate. All sorts of people start businesses, and all sorts of people thrive after doing so. There is no such thing as an identikit entrepreneur. The only difference between those who've succeeded already and you is that they've chosen to deploy the same tools that you have in your possession in pursuit of their own dream, and not someone else's. We blame popular misconceptions on what we call the 'Richard Branson effect'. One look at him ballooning spectacularly around the world and you probably feel that deep down inside, someone like you hasn't got what it takes. You believe entrepreneurship requires an alchemist's formula reserved for the genius. Well, here's the good news: it doesn't! As surely as not every successful business is like Virgin, so every successful (and happy) entrepreneur does not need to have Bransonesque personal qualities to make their vision work.

Look around your local high street and most of the retail brands around you were once upon a time nothing more than entrepreneurial start-ups. What you don't see is that the faces behind these start-ups were not business prodigies. Most of them knew nothing about business and few of them ever set out to become 'entrepreneurs'. They just knew and loved their products, and their businesses were built on the back of their dedication to an ideal.

History is rich with entrepreneurs of all shapes and sizes. If you think about it, Christopher Columbus is one early example. His great idea was to find a faster route to Asia by sailing westwards instead of to the east and therefore making trade more profitable in the process. On the way he discovered America! It took Columbus six years to persuade King Ferdinand of Spain through his 'business plan' to finance his expedition.

Once Columbus got royal support and financial backing he bought ships, hired men (his 'management team') and set sail six months later ('establishing his business').

One hundred years after Columbus the first colonists had another great idea: go to America to tap the new market for gold, silver and jewels. Our unwary explorers faced the same task of any entrepreneur, that of finding funding for the venture either from the crown or a trading company. And so they, too, set sail into uncharted territories to establish their businesses. We think of these people as pioneers but their activities are really the root of what we call entrepreneurship today.

History is littered with successful people who recognised an opportunity and acted on it. They are all entrepreneurs. The word 'entrepreneur' itself may be an invention of our times, but the reality is as old as humanity.

Law 2: Entrepreneurship is not a personality trait

The thing to understand is that there is no universal entre-preneurial type. There is no one set of common characteristics that can somehow define in advance whether, if you share those characteristics, your business is more likely to succeed. In entrepreneurship, we are talking about a 'discipline' that all people can learn. It is bred, not born.

In the words of the entrepreneurship guru Peter Drucker: *"It is not a personality trait: In thirty years I have seen people of most diverse personalities and temperaments perform well in entrepreneurial challenges. Some entrepreneurs are egocentric and others are painfully correct conformists. Some are fat and some are lean. Some entrepreneurs are worriers and some are relaxed…some have great charm and some have no more personality than a frozen mackerel!"*

Peter Drucker's wife started her own business at the age of 80 when she saw a gap in the hearing aids market. How untypical is that?

A good answer we've heard to the question 'what is an entrepreneur?' is this: it's like an elephant. It's difficult to describe but you'll know one when you see one!

So the best and perhaps only definition that truly describes and captures all entrepreneurs is that they act in fundamentally the same way: they start and operate their own business. More widely, they identify an opportunity and have the courage to act on it.

Law 3: Behaving like an entrepreneur is a process anyone can learn

Since there is no one entrepreneurial personality type, anyone can take the actions and master the skills that will make them an entrepreneur. Peter Drucker notes that "anyone who can face up to decision making can learn to be an entrepreneur and behave entrepreneurially. Entrepreneurship is a behaviour rather than a personality trait."

We believe that once you have an idea and decide to pursue it, you start behaving entrepreneurially without even realising it. The one common denominator that all entrepreneurs share is a dream and a willingness to do whatever it takes to turn that dream into a reality. You visualise an end product and work backwards to make it happen.

It's also worth stressing that entrepreneurs are different from inventors. Inventors are the geniuses that come up with ideas while entrepreneurs make a business out of ideas (often those of other people). Inventors rely on their instinct and genius. They are the Thomas Edisons of this world and there are only a handful of them. Entrepreneurs, on the other hand, follow a process that may be intuitive to some but can be learned by all.

All entrepreneurs go through basically the same process of taking the grain of an idea through to becoming an operating business. The steps involved are fairly straightforward and we cover these in the rest of this book (market research, business plan, raising money, implementation).

By following the process as you start, you can learn to behave entrepreneurially using tools we all have within us. Those tools are hard work, commitment, persistence and determination. All entrepreneurs rely on them. But the tools need to be activated. Your passion for your idea is what will do this.

Once that's happened, you will start behaving entrepreneurially in every aspect of you life, not just in business. You will start being more proactive in making sure the things you really want are within your reach. You will refuse to take 'no' for an answer on almost any issue.

Law 4: Passion will activate your entrepreneurial qualities

It's your fuel! A core prerequisite for behaving like an entrepreneur is having passion for your business idea. The 'entrepreneur within' will be activated through passion. So the key to bringing out the entrepreneur within you is getting as close as possible to something you can get passionate about. If you do, then passion becomes the fuel for your entrepreneurial journey; 'it makes the world go round'. That fire in your stomach will bring out all the qualities that you already have, but need to activate.

If the idea doesn't turn you on, you will find it very hard to motivate yourself to do all the hard work and overcome all the obstacles. If you don't love what you do, the long, arduous journey just won't be worth it. Hard work will just feel like hard work rather than something you just do as you pursue your dream. You are better off working nine to five.

Passion, in short, is what makes you behave entrepreneurially and triggers all the qualities you need along the way. Every single entrepreneur's story starts with the passion for an idea. And anyone can find something they can get passionate about.

Law 5: You don't need skills or expertise

You might be surprised to learn that the majority of entrepreneurs were neither trained nor experienced in the field in which they launched their business. In fact most of them didn't have any serious business experience at all (like actually running a company) when they started out.

It seems that starting their business taught them everything they needed to know as they went along. The act of start-up, in other words, becomes the entrepreneur's greatest source of learning. It's a business school, located bang in the middle of the real world.

When we started to write our first business plan, Sahar believed that she couldn't succeed without getting an MBA. To which Bobby replied, "Sahar, you're about to go to the best business school in the world."

Sometimes, in fact, the lack of deep industry experience and knowledge acts to the entrepreneur's advantage. We call it 'the importance of being clueless' as this allows you to think only of the end product and to be blissfully unaware of the obstacles along the way. Conventional thinking forces you to think 'in the box' and as an entrepreneur you need 'out of the box' thinking. Your lack of deep industry background thus gives you the open mindedness you need to manage the uncertainty that others necessarily won't, and to work to achieve your goal.

That is not to say that you can get by without assessing your strengths and weaknesses. As you go along you should always try to learn the skills you need. Some you can teach yourself, for others you can hire people or use professionals to help you. Either way, you have to be realistic in your self-appraisal.

Law 6: Anyone can do it – but does everyone want to? Is entrepreneurship your sort of thing?

Although anyone can do it, we are not saying that starting a business is for everybody. You have to ask yourself the fundamental question: Am I sure that I really want to be an entrepreneur? It's wise to think long and hard about whether you want to embark on the journey. It's not a simple career choice. Starting a business is as much a personal concept as a business one. It's a lifestyle as much as a career.

It's something that reflects not just what you do, but also who you are. For entrepreneurs the two are often the same thing. They integrate their personal interests with their work. That is a double-edged sword. On the plus side you are doing something that fits you as an individual, you love it and you control your destiny. On the minus side, it brings huge uncertainty into your life and you can't ever shut off. At the beginning, at least, you and your business are one. That is an emotional commitment you have to be ready for.

An entrepreneur friend once told us "Starting a business is no different than starting anything else. The opportunity it presents as a path to self-realisation is one most often overlooked. Ultimately I feel this is its greatest benefit." We really believe that if measured in terms of self-realisation, every entrepreneur makes billions out of the journey itself, regardless of their degree of measurable success.

Law 7: Warning: success is not all that easy to come by. The failure rate is 99%

"Many people dream of success. To me success can only be achieved through repeated failure and introspection. In fact, success represents one percent of your work which results from the 99 percent that is called failure." - S. HONDA, JAPANESE INDUSTRIALIST

The process of entrepreneurship is an enormously time and soul consuming project. Being an entrepreneur is hard work. You'll hear more rejections and discouragement than you could imagine, and you'll have to keep going in spite of the critics. And the critics will greet you at every turn. It will take longer to achieve your dreams than you think or hope. Everything that you dread might happen will almost certainly happen along the way. Nothing you do want to happen will happen easily. Every entrepreneur says that they had no idea at the beginning how difficult it would be.

But if you do go for it, we promise that it will be the best thing you will do in your life. None of those entrepreneurs who confronted the realities regret that they did so. With hindsight, they loved every minute of it. Most of them are almost nostalgic for the old days. Looking back, the hardships and the uphill climbs all seem so romantic now. MUCH LIG PUBLIC ACOOUNTING

"I wish I could be who I was when I wanted to be who I am now."

Stay hungry

Law 8: So decide for yourself what to do. You have to make the decision and only you can do it

There is nothing honourable about being an entrepreneur or dishonourable about working for someone else. It's all about what YOU want from your life and from your day. Entrepreneurship has got to be your kind of thing.

We suggest that you consider whether or not to proceed very carefully. Ignore books and entrepreneur checklists that ask questions like: Do you love failure? Do you anticipate rejections with glee? Do you have amazing leadership qualities? Are you super-creative? Are you exceptionally charismatic and good with people?

Such books are designed to reinforce the conventional image of the entrepreneur as a superhuman icon. They subtly suggest that not just anyone can be a successful entrepreneur. How, after all, can anyone love failure? How can you tell whether you're creative if you have studied law and worked in a law firm all your life, as Sahar did? How can you be a good leader if you've never been given the chance to lead?

The point about entrepreneurship is that with the fuel of passion in your tank, you will discover qualities that you never knew existed within you. If you were previously in a lacklustre job in an environment you hated then it stands to reason that you would be out of touch with the positive parts of your personality and might therefore lack self-belief.

But starting a business requires a more conscious decision than applying for a job. There are no recruiters or corporate headhunters. Since you can't go for a job interview, you have to interview yourself. Here are questions you can ask yourself before you embark on the journey.

INTERVIEW YOURSELF: IS ENTREPRENEURSHIP FOR YOU?

☐ Are you ready to commit yourself entirely to get your idea off the ground?

☐ Is your personal life ready for you committing to your business?

☐ Do you have other responsibilities that prevent you committing to your new idea?

☐ Do you have enough staying power to keep at it until it works? Assume that it will always take longer than you expect.

☐ Are you willing to work extremely hard?

☐ Are you ready to say 'no' back when others say 'no' to you?

☐ Are you ready to roll up your sleeves and do everything yourself – however menial the task? Entrepreneurship is not about ideas alone.

☐ Do you have a deep, burning passion to make your idea work?

If your answer to these questions is "yes", then you possess the seed of the secret ingredient you'll need to become a successful entrepreneur and create the life of your dreams. You show the first symptoms of commitment.

Law 9: You can't be a half-hearted entrepreneur

We don't believe in toe-dipping in entrepreneurship. You need to commit to it. We know that phrase sounds more than a little overused. Let's face it – everyone talks about commitment. But don't ignore commitment because it's become a cliché. It really is a key ingredient for success.

On the road between your great idea and your viable business lies a minefield of fears, obstacles, rejections and discouragements. The only way to make it through this minefield and the barriers within is commitment.

If passion is your fuel, commitment is your engine. It gives you the driving force to make it through the barriers and get to your destination. The stronger your passion, the more revved up your engine; that is what will steer you through the obstacles ahead, sometimes without even realising it. Once you are committed, little can stop you from achieving your goals.

"Until one is committed there is hesitancy, the chance to draw back, always ineffectiveness. Concerning all acts of initiative there is one elementary truth the ignorance of which kills countless ideas and endless plans: the moment you definitely commit yourself, then Providence moves. All sorts of things occur that would never otherwise have occurred. A whole stream of events issue from the decision, raising in your favour all manner of unseen incidents and meetings and material assistance, which you could never have dreamed would come your way. Whatever you can do or dream, you can. Begin it. Boldness has genius, power, magic to it."
- GOETHE

The great thing about commitment is that it exists on an ever-increasing curve. Don't expect to be fully committed at the outset.

We will explain in Chapter 3 how, as you begin to work on turning your idea into a reality, you will get more and more committed. But at this stage all you need is the commitment to being an entrepreneur.

Law 10: Don't bother if you're just in it for the cash

Wanting to get rich isn't a good enough reason to start a business. Although the best way to make a fortune is to start your own business it should not be why you do it. If money is your only motivation, your business will almost certainly fail.

If you look at most entrepreneurs who have made a fortune it has been a result of achieving a specific non-financial goal. Bill Gates' mission statement was never 'to be the richest man in the world'. It was actually 'a PC on every desk and in every home'.

Our father taught us this maxim: "Don't chase after money. Let money chase after you." If you have a great idea and you're committed to implementing it the money will indeed chase after you.

"I usually can tell the difference between people who have that fire in their stomachs and those who see ideas primarily to get rich. I'm looking for entrepreneurs who ask 'how can I make this business a success?' not 'how do I make a fortune?"

- ARTHUR ROCK, *Harvard Business Review*

FORGET ABOUT IT:
Entrepreneurship is definitely not for you if:

- [ ] You actually enjoy the structure of working nine to five.
- [ ] You want a clear divide between your life and your work.
- [ ] You hate responsibility.
- [ ] You can't cope with uncertainty.
- [ ] A 'no' puts you off.
- [ ] You are lazy and proud of it!

PLUSES AND MINUSES OF BEING AN ENTREPRENEUR:

+ Flexible working hours.	– A 24-hour-a-day job.
+ You love what you do.	– You're not getting paid for it at the beginning.
+ You are your own boss.	– You are responsible for others.
+ No more office politics.	– You're quite lonely.
+ No more commuting.	– You'll have all the mundane chores.
+ You can work from home.	– Home will no longer be relaxing.
+ It's fun and fulfilling to follow your dream.	– Selling your dream is a real uphill struggle with uncertainty

Our Story – how we got here

S o far we have tried to prove that 'anyone can do it' and that you don't have to have superhuman qualities to make things work. In taking this approach, we believe that we represent a new breed of entrepreneur who doesn't fit the image from central casting. We were not born entrepreneurs. Instead, certain circumstances conspired to make us entrepreneurs. Here is how we came to our journey.

We are siblings. There are four years in age between us, with Bobby being the older.

Entrepreneurship wasn't in our genes. We don't come from a family of entrepreneurs. Our father was a corporate executive. Our mother was a full-time devoted mother. We have no connection whatsoever with retail, food brands or coffee in any shape or form. If anything, we are quite the reverse of the apocryphal entrepreneur who dropped out of school but whose genius could nevertheless not be constrained. We followed the path of education according to convention and instead of learning the laws of supply and demand by trading in the school playground, we spent the time playing instead. We were frighteningly average people.

We were in no way exceptional. Neither of us were overachievers or under-achievers either at school or in our hobbies. We didn't necessarily stand out as having amazing talents or particular brilliance in anything requiring us to use our imaginations.

Sahar's dog (aged 9)

Creative is something we were not. We were horribly 'normal' and to give you an example of our lack of creativity, we were both notoriously bad at drawing. In one art class, Sahar was asked to draw her dog and, after seeing the result, her teacher was left wondering if she really kept a Tyrannosaurus Rex at home!

We didn't show any business flair in childhood. We didn't earn a penny in Machiavellian ways. The thought of selling sweets or worms never even crossed our minds. Sahar's only commercial venture was selling Christmas trees door-to-door for charity. The first time either of us made any money was at university during summer internships: Sahar at a law firm, Bobby at an investment bank.

Not only were we not brought up to be entrepreneurs, we were taught to study 'useful subjects' and aim for a solid profession. So Bobby studied computer engineering and Sahar studied law.

If we got any training for entrepreneurship in our upbringing, then it was being taught the value of discipline and hard work. We were taught that the key to success was not a matter of inspiration but rather 'it's all about the perspiration.' What you put into something determines what you get out. Our parents' maxim was 'it's not about being the best, it's about doing your best.' They believed that if you put your head down, worked hard and persisted, you could achieve anything. That is the most important lesson we were ever taught.

Our other home advantage was that we were taught the value of having dreams. They are the seedlings of reality. Since the ages of twelve, Sahar knew that she wanted to be a lawyer and Bobby a financier.

We'll now fast-forward to adulthood...

 NEW YORK 1993

Bobby was working at Lehman Brothers Investment Banking, New York in the Mergers & Acquisitions department. He had always wanted to be a Wall Street investment banker working in exactly the type of place in which he found himself and living exactly the type of life he actually lived.

Bobby was persuaded to study computer engineering at university by our father, who felt it was the profession of the future and, truth be told, he hated every minute of it! Nevertheless, he never considered giving up his course for a minute. That said, when he finished his degree Bobby wanted to nothing more to do with the subject, preferring to return to his goal of joining the world of finance and business.

He started dabbling in the stock market the summer he graduated from university and with a few lucky hunches he quickly made some sound investments. He therefore boasted to our father that there was a quicker way to make money than working hard in an office. To teach him a lesson our father gave him £10,000 and challenged him to increase the sum ten fold over the summer. Within ten days Bobby had managed to lose it all, a lesson in humility and reality that he puts down as the most valuable he's ever learned – there's no such thing as easy money; you have to earn it.

He really discovered his true passion during his time studying for an MBA at Tuck Business School in Dartmouth, New Hampshire. It was two stimulating years of hard study and sturdy outdoor sports activities in the Vermont countryside, following which he joined Lehman Brothers. Bobby's lifestyle there was classic eighties New York, working all night more frequently than having a good night's sleep. His endurance record was working on a deal from 7 a.m. one Thursday morning right through until Monday morning with two red-eye flights thrown in for good measure!

Sahar came to visit him in New York one weekend but she never saw him as he didn't leave his office for two entire days except to come home once at 3 a.m. to change shirts – it was that gruelling. In fact, the monstrously disciplined investment banker played by Sigourney Weaver in the movie, *Working Girl* was based on Bobby's boss.

Still, these were also the heady days of investment banking. It was the *Bonfire of the Vanities* era. These were the times of company expense accounts and unashamed indulgence.

All of Bobby's friends were investment bankers. From within his cocoon the high life seemed normal and invigorating, save for a slight discomfort around bonus time that usually soon eased with the receipt of a six-figure cheque to erase the memories of the all nighters and temporarily replace them with new dreams of untold riches. It sounds extreme, but Bobby's life was typical of its kind.

Bobby and his friends would often sit in the oak-panelled boardrooms of New York dreaming of one day starting their own companies. They all had plenty of ideas they had carried in their hearts since business school; after all, most of them had read nearly every business biography ever written and they had all spent a lifetime training for entrepreneurship.

The only question in the minds of Bobby and his friends was when they would do it. The answer was always 'not today' as their dreams would be constantly interrupted by the demands of the high-powered deals they were shuffling.

Whether you're a high-flying investment banker or in a nine to five job that gives you little pleasure, the initial problem with entrepreneurship is the same: will you be able to find the courage to leave the safety of a reliable working life and start over for yourself with all the risk which that entails?

Unless they were 100% – or even 105% – sure that it was going to work, Bobby and his friends were never quite prepared to make the move.

LONDON 1993

At the same time as Bobby was working in New York, Sahar was a lawyer at the prestigious law firm of Frere Cholmeley in Lincoln's Inn Fields, London. It had been Sahar's dream to work there from the first moment she went to their presentation at Bristol University. Instead of the pasty-faced lawyers other firms sent out to recruit undergraduates, Frere Cholmeley had sent a more impressive collection of lawyers than even the producers of Ally McBeal might be able to muster. The firm represented almost all the leading names in the entertainment industry, and had offices in Paris and Monaco (as opposed to the more boring locations where law firms normally have offices). On top of that, they seemed to know how to enjoy life as well as work. For Sahar, the choice was instinctive.

What Sahar likes to forget now and again is that Frere Cholmeley rejected her three times (she applied to them twice for summer placements in her first and second years). But she didn't give up. She eased down on the university partying in her third year (after all, she had done it non-stop for two years) and cranked up on her studies, finally getting the required grades. She reapplied and got the job offer she wanted; her dream came true!

At first after she joined the firm, Frere Cholmeley totally lived up to Sahar's expectations. Her new colleagues worked hard and they played harder. Her strict regime of hard work during the last year of Bristol and the gruelling year of Law Society finals at Chancery Lane were worth it. Just as Bobby worked in investment banking's glory days, so Sahar's stint in the corridors of the law corresponded with a golden period of big deals, power suits, and the inexorable rise of the glamorous female lawyer. The skirts were short, the heels were high, and the shoulder pads could knock an American footballer over. The female partners were inspirational role models, and she thought she had found true professional happiness.

It got even better when Sahar was sent to Paris for six months, staying at the immense company apartments in the Marais and working from offices in a palatial building in Trocadero, overlooking the Eiffel Tower.

The first two years post law school are called 'articles', an on-the-job training period in which the fledging lawyer becomes a fullyfledged attorney. At this time the trainee is required to work six months in each department of the firm. Having returned from her Paris sojourn, Sahar was assigned to the litigation department where things got even better.

She was placed on the case dealing with Arthur Scargill. For those unfamiliar with him, he was head of the Miners' Union that almost brought down Margaret Thatcher's government during the infamous Miners' Strike of the 1980s. To cut a long story short, on a balmy day in July 1989 Sahar was plastered all over the nation's TV screens and tabloid newspapers as the glamorous mini-skirted lawyer who served a writ on the great socialist himself. Her 15 minutes of legal fame had happened before she'd even completed her articles!

After actually qualifying as a lawyer though, everything started to change. Frere Cholmeley offered her a much-coveted place in its prestigious entertainment group where Sahar found that apart from the group's name, there wasn't much entertainment going on. Being a lawyer was very different from being a trainee lawyer.

As a trainee you swanned in and out of departments and sections – a fast-paced existence long on excitement and short on drudgery. If you didn't like things, you knew that you would be moving on to your next post soon enough. You would look good at meetings basking in the greatness of the senior lawyer to whom you were 'articled' for that week. Being a trainee lawyer you felt as if you were the best lawyer Britain had ever produced; almost by osmosis you took on the skills of the lawyers around you. In short, you had a manageable work load, no pressure, lots of reward, and even more fun.

All that changes when you qualify as a lawyer. The music stops and you find yourself sitting in one chair behind one desk permanently. It amounts to payback time for all the glory you enjoyed as a trainee. The meetings, the fun and the glamour come to an abrupt end. Sahar spent her time drafting documents – and the longer the document the better for the firm. She swears now that she did not meet anyone or even leave her office for her first four months in the job proper. She was imprisoned in a room with only a post box for company; documents to process were slipped under her door and had to come back out with Sahar's contribution included.

"No, no, NO," she screamed to herself. Rapidly she decided that this was not the life for her. She would visit the offices of her peers lamenting the unimaginative nature of the work and being nostalgic for the good old days. She searched for university friends who had found their true vocation outside the law. But she found that they all loved the complex nitty-gritty of the legal world. She was alone in her chagrin.

One day in the depths of desperation and with a complex joint venture agreement taking up her time, a light bulb went on in Sahar's head. She had found a way out. Having espied a group of glamorous American lawyers from the prestigious New York law firm Skadden Arps in the office, and having heard that one of the senior lawyers was returning from his secondment there, Sahar approached the partner in question with the solution to her quest for legal bliss. Although she acknowledged that she was aware that lawyers were not eligible for the New York place until their fourth year, she was ready for it immediately. She was ejected from the partner's office even more swiftly than she'd entered, with the result that she could barely utter the words "New York" for months to come.

So the disillusionment of the naturally enthusiastic Sahar snowballed as days went by. Her intuition was telling her that she was not happy as a lawyer – but she didn't want to listen to her negative inner voice, especially after so much hard work. How could she possibly not be a lawyer when it was a longstanding ambition for which she had studied all her life?

Then suddenly everything changed…

In a moment, both our worlds were turned upside down. A life-changing moment.

On the night of 23 January 1993 our close-knit family of four was shattered with the sudden death of our father from a stroke at the age of sixty-two.

Earlier that day Bobby had enjoyed a wonderful phone conversation from New York with his father in London who was on great form as usual and was starting to get used to his new life in retirement.

Sahar made the dreaded call to Bobby at midnight from a London hospital explaining that their dad had passed away peacefully, and Bobby just managed to take the last British Airways flight out of New York. He never really went back to New York after that.

Our father's sudden death was a paradigm shift for both of us. It was the sort of event that shakes up every single supposition or plan you've ever made – the sort of shock that sees you putting on new lenses and looking at the world in a totally different light, where nothing that came before matters in the slightest way. The loss of a parent strips you from your comfort zone, making other drastic changes you once considered too risky much easier to undertake.

For Bobby, the investment banking routine lost its meaning. While his gruelling work schedule had not given him time to consider the life he wanted, he realised he needed to be closer to his mother and sister and the work schedule would never allow that if he stayed at Lehman. Lehman Brothers understood his predicament and, proving itself to be a truly great employer, gave Bobby a six month sabbatical followed by a transfer to London.

Sahar remained at her law firm for one more year but realised that being a lawyer was not going to make her happy in life. At first she thought that the solution to her career dilemma was to become an in-house lawyer for a major company. "I want to be close to the fruits of my labour," she used to repeat at interviews explaining why she wanted to go in-house, along with "I want my life and my work to mix". Sahar would relate being a lawyer to the following scenario: the client is the host inviting the guests, choosing the menu and entertaining while the lawyer is in the kitchen chopping the carrots and washing up but never getting to attend the dinner.

She thought being an in-house lawyer would solve this problem because you do feel more involved, and you do get invited to the feast. But although she was being interviewed by lots of companies Sahar never received a job offer. Now, of course, she knows why: in-house lawyers should be marked, measured, cautious and very prudent. She was none of those things and, to make it worse, she spoke and thought at breakneck speed. She was applying, in short, for a job totally ill-suited to her personality.

We had 'lost sight of the shore only to discover a new ocean'.

By January 1994, Sahar had decided to give herself a well-deserved break and pursue her ambition to take the gap year she had overlooked after graduation to go to Argentina and learn Spanish. This period ended up lasting four months. Having had an amazingly refreshing break on the Pampas, trekking the Andes on horseback and learning a decent amount of Spanish, she felt recharged, reprogrammed and ready to get back to London.

By the end of 1994 what we both didn't realise was that we had subconsciously made the big break from our comfort zones. We had cut the umbilical cord. Although we spent 1993 in a bit of a daze during a year of mixed emotions, questions, and ups and downs, by the end of 1994 we were fairly restored. We had made the changes in our personal outlooks that we had needed to make. Changes which had it not been for our father's death we probably would never have made.

Our time off also gave us time to clarify what we wanted out of life and our careers. Little did we know that by leaving the comfort zone and really thinking about our personal and career goals we had taken the first step in the journey of entrepreneurship. The truth is that we never thought for a moment that we would end up working together, let alone starting a business together. But you don't need a life-changing crisis to inspire the changes that you need to make. If you are unhappy with your status quo you can choose to leave your comfort zone at any time. The key is to be proactive. Don't rely exclusively on your left-brain capacity, which is the logical rational side. You need to tap into your rightbrain capacity, where creativity and intuition reside, to enable you to visualize what you want to do and to be in life.

"I never discovered anything with my rational mind."
- ALBERT EINSTEIN

CHAPTER TWO:
THE IDEA CHAPTER
DO YOU HAVE A LIGHT BULB, OR DO YOU NEED TO FIND ONE?

If you've decided that the entrepreneurial life is for you, you can now move on to the next stage. But remember that a restless itch to do your own thing is not enough to ensure your future success. Before anything else, you need to work out what you are going to do. Exactly what business do you want to start?

In some ways, you'll face what will seem to be a bit of a chicken and egg dilemma. Does the idea come first, with the business itself to follow? Or can you decide to do things in reverse: determine to start working for yourself and then discover the business that gives you the best opportunity for success? Either the idea 'light bulb' itself will be what drives you forward, or it will simply be your burning desire to become an entrepreneur.

Fortunately, entrepreneurship can start along either path.

Our definition of a light bulb (the idea you need at the core of your business) is this: an idea which fills a gap in the market and that you passionately believe you can act upon successfully. There's nothing complicated about this. You just need to find something about which you feel so passionately that it will trigger the entrepreneur within!

Either way, whether you already have your idea or you've decided to look for one, here are the rules defining good ideas that we've learned and that we think you would do well to follow.

Law 11: Your idea doesn't need to be new, original or revolutionary

Do you think that to become a successful entrepreneur, you have to be ground-breakingly original? If you do, you're wrong. That's good news, because the likelihood that you'll have an idea that is both totally new and completely functional is not very high. In fact, it's almost zero unless you're Thomas Edison, but we'll come to that later.   *Like the iPad*

Most entrepreneurs start their businesses by copying or slightly modifying someone else's idea. Being the first is not always best, a fact known as the 'first mover disadvantage.' Selling a totally new product will almost always be an uphill struggle because you have to establish the concept from scratch and educate the market, rather than simply capitalising on existing and proven demand. Believe us when we tell you that there is nothing more expensive than educating a market.

Of course it also does not follow that you can offer something identical to that provided by another business. The key is the opportunity you see for your idea and the determination that you have to make it work better or more cheaply or be different from what anyone else is already doing. Your idea has to have a USP, a unique selling point that distinguishes it in the market.

Law 12: Remember that entrepreneurs are different from inventors

Always remember that you're not an inventor, but an entrepreneur. As an entrepreneur you don't need to invent an idea. Entrepreneurs simply make businesses out of ideas that for the most part already exist. Inventors are creative geniuses who come up with new things.

There are few inventors turned entrepreneurs, the best-known exception to this rule being James Dyson: he is both the inventor of and the entrepreneur behind his product. For the most part, entrepreneurs merely exploit the ideas capital that inventors leave behind.

Law 13: Be your own first customer

While you are at the light bulb stage, be certain to make sure that you approach your business idea from the perspective of the customer and not as the 'seller'. Don't think of yourself and your customers as 'us' and 'them'.

It's easy and tempting to make that mistake but it is not helpful to have a divide in your own mind between you as the seller and 'them' as customers when you're thinking about your business.

If you can't convince yourself to buy your product and you haven't found a first customer elsewhere then don't bother proceeding. However much money you throw at your idea through marketing and advertising, it won't sell. In that case, the customer is not out there. Customers are not a body of people you can fool or cajole into buying your product. You are the customer yourself.

Your life will be much easier if you think along these lines and you will save yourself thousands of pounds (which, in any event, you are unlikely to have available at the start) on customer surveys as well. The key is that if you would buy your product, and you can find another twenty people who would do the same, then it WILL sell.

Law 14: Don't approach your idea with money in mind. Money doesn't turn on your light bulb!

The question NOT to ask at the light bulb stage is 'how can I make money?' You will address whether your idea will make money at the next stage of the process of launching a business. For the present, at the very start, you should look at profit like a dessert at the end of the meal and not let your desire for untold riches hamper your creativity. Good ideas make money, but you don't have to chase after it. Let the money chase after you.

If you approach an idea with only future riches in mind (and if you did, you wouldn't be the first) then you're not an entrepreneur. Instead, you're a bandwagon jumper. And we have seen more than a bit of a bandwagon jumping in our business. It's a trap a lot of budding entrepreneurs have fallen into, to their cost.

The problem with bandwagon jumping is that there is no belief in what's behind the business. Such businesses weren't started to follow a burning urge to do something better than already existed, or to fill a gap in the market. They were created to merely try and surf a passing wave. The thought of being the 'next Pret A Manger' (and a lot of people wanted to be exactly that) was more exciting than the products being sold. That's why only a few of these businesses have survived. Most of them didn't even last a year. They weren't built on a foundation of passion, but rather one of greed.

The recent dot.com burst is a good example of bandwagon jumping. A lot of dot.com ideas were based solely on the money making angle. Internet entrepreneurs saw the Internet as a great way to make fast profits and not as a genuine opportunity to meet a need in the market. They therefore approached things from the wrong angle. The only businesses that have survived on the Internet are those like Amazon that were founded with genuine passion for a market opportunity, in that case selling books.

Law 15: Make sure the business idea suits you

When you're coming up with an idea, the first judge it faces is you. Take your own opinion seriously! The business needs to fit your personality because, especially at the beginning, it's really an extension of you. So, if you're not a people person, don't go into a services business and if you hate being desk-bound, don't start a business that will chain you to an office.

If you don't have a light bulb idea already and you want to start up on your own you should keep searching until an idea comes to you. Just keep thinking about the things you love doing and use your creative imagination. Anything can give you an idea: working,

BRAINSTORMING SESSION

Here are some ideas to help you prepare for a productive brainstorming session. Don't get too intense when trying to find a good business idea or you will stifle your creativity. It is important to have your right brain (the intuitive and creative as opposed to the logical side) working if you want to find a great idea. So:

☐ Get four or five friends from different backgrounds and with different interests together.

☐ Make the environment cosy and comfortable. Put on some music.

☐ Get the creative juices flowing and don't be in a business mindset.

☐ Don't discount any idea, however ridiculous it seems. Have fun!

HOW TO FIND A LIGHT BULB

☐ **What do you love in life?**
What matters to you?
What hobbies do you have?
What do you enjoy doing?
What is the favourite part of your day?

☐ **Is there any way you can improve on something familiar?**
Have you seen anything abroad that would make a difference to your life at work or at home?
Have you thought of a better way of delivering/producing something that matters to you than already exists?

☐ **Is there an obvious gap in the market?**
Is there something you love that you can't find?
Is there a product/service that would make a big difference in your life?

☐ **Do you have a skill or expertise you can capitalise on?**
Is there a product/service that you particularly know a lot about?
Do you know of a different way of offering something?
Do you have a skill that you would love to put to better use?

Questions not to ask yourself at the idea stage:
☐ How can I make money quickly?

shopping, travelling, reading or talking to friends. It's also useful to have a brainstorming session to help you along your way.

How entrepreneurs have found their ideas.
Here are some examples of the varying inspirations behind some entrepreneurial starts-ups:

- Founder had left Christmas shopping too late and couldn't find the last-minute gadgets he wanted.
  Resulting idea: GADGET SHOP

- Founder discovered market opportunity to sell mobile phones direct to consumers.
  Resulting idea: CARPHONE WAREHOUSE

- Founder's wife cried after optician said she had to wait seven days for new glasses.
  Resulting idea: VISION EXPRESS

- Founder had a passion for making scents and lotions.
  The name: JO MALONE

As you can see, each of these businesses has its roots in circumstance. The ideas were not deliberately conceived as much as they fell into the founders' laps because they were alert to an opportunity. These entrepreneurs let the idea come to them.

Our Story – how we got our idea

4 NOVEMBER 1994

To recap on where we were when we left our story in the last chapter, Sahar had departed from her law firm, returned from her travels and had been searching unsuccessfully for an in-house legal position for which she was probably ill-suited.

Bobby had decided not to go back to Lehman after his sabbatical period ended and was looking at options for starting his own business.

So we were both floating in the middle of a somewhat broad ocean, neither possessed of any particular direction and with no sign of the shore in sight. In the back of our minds, the alarm bells were starting to ring. What on earth were we going to do?

Our 'light bulb' night

On the night of 4 November 1994, Sahar was feeling utterly despondent about her inability to find the job she wanted so she went to an evening seminar at Café Royale given by a firm of legal headhunters. You know the sort of event, and the somewhat desperate stage of life you have to be at to want to attend that sort of function in person! Everyone dressed in full job seeking regalia, determined to both stand out and not stand in the crowd, and obsessively trying to say the right thing. And everyone fighting for the same position though many are not quite sure why.

If Sahar felt desperate beforehand, by the end of the seminar she felt even worse. She found that after her mind-broadening travels, she now fitted into the corporate environment even less. Looking around her, she did not feel she was seeing a future she really wanted.

Bobby had agreed to collect her afterwards to go out for a Thai meal at Boosabong, just off the King's Road, with our mother. Sahar got into the car feeling totally deflated but as she closed the door she could sense an overpoweringly positive energy from Bobby. Bobby was beaming with a business idea. Or, in the Zen sense, the Idea had taken hold of him. He was totally engaged in the process of developing the Idea in his mind, though Sahar didn't even know what it was.

Basically, on her way back from Argentina, Sahar had stopped in New York for a couple of weeks and being an early riser she had become used to going to a coffee bar called New World Coffee on Madison and 44th Street.

There she experienced for the first time a specialty coffee bar with its skinny cappuccinos (a real novelty at the time) and fat-free carrot muffins (also previously unknown) and everything else that made the experience seem like a haven of luxury in the hustle and bustle of the day.

When Sahar returned from New York, she raved on to Bobby about how totally in love she was with these incredible coffee bars in New York, and how much she missed them already and how much she wished they had the same thing in London. She was speaking, of course, only as a consumer.

As Sahar was enthusing on the subject, somewhere in the back of his mind Bobby remembered that an ex-colleague had put the prospectus of a budding US coffee chain on his desk at Lehman at one point, bringing to his attention the enormous coffeedrinking boom occurring in the USA.

Then, with these thoughts logged somewhere in the recesses of his subconscious, on that very day he had been out to several meetings and had been shocked to realise that you could not stop off for an even half-way decent cup of coffee anywhere in London. Bobby couldn't help but think back to what Sahar had said. She was right!

So Bobby got the Idea. The light bulb in his head turned itself on and the first step on the road to entrepreneurship was almost subconsciously taken. He was determined that he and Sahar should start up a chain of US-style coffee bars in London.

Sahar protested vehemently about any involvement from her. "Why are you discussing business with me," she asked, "when you know that I have no interest whatsoever in it? I only liked the coffee bars as a customer." She suddenly felt incredibly anxious and insecure at the thought of giving up her hard-earned experience and qualification as a lawyer to go into the world of coffee bars.

Bobby, however, managed to persuade her that he would pay her to do the research on his idea for one week only, and added that it would be her decision whether to move the idea ahead or not. Sahar, weighing the thought of another demoralising week of job interviews against having enough cash to buy a Prada coat, and showing a keen sense for the right motivation, agreed to Bobby's proposal.

The next morning she walked to High Street Kensington tube station, bought a one-day travel pass, and circumnavigated the Circle Line getting off at every single one of the 27 stops. She went around a two-block radius of each tube station to inspect what was on offer to the commuter in search of a cup of coffee.

In some ways, Sahar loved what she saw. There was obviously a huge demand for coffee, though the product itself was horrible. Queues at sandwich bars for coffee, queues at fast food outlets for coffee, queues at kiosks for coffee. And when you could get your hands on a cup, the product being served was essentially brown sludge in a grubby polystyrene cup covered by an ill-fitting lid (which, thankfully, is now a distant memory for most of us).

Sahar remembered from her legal days how important the

morning cappuccino was. It occurred to her that the reason the coffee was so poor was because all the outlets she visited were essentially focused on other products. Those sandwich bars were really in the business of making egg mayo rolls; coffee was very much a sideline.

Nevertheless, it was obvious that coffee was sold in huge quantities.

Sahar could not believe how strongly she felt that day, and she realised that there was an enormous gap in the market for a high-quality coffee experience where the main focus was on the quality of your coffee drink and not on anything else.

So a light bulb also turned on for Sahar. London was missing out on the New York-style coffee experience and we could significantly enhance the quality of London's caffeine habit if we provided it. In terms of buying into Bobby's idea, that was pretty much that. Sahar was in, and that was the minute that Coffee Republic was born.

FACSIMILE: 10:00PM, 5 NOVEMBER 1994

Bobby,

I CANNOT believe what I saw today on my Circle Line trip. I had honestly forgotten since my lawyer days how totally grim the take-away offer is. London SO desperately needs NY style espresso bars!!

This is how I've summed up the status quo:

- You leave the tube station on your way to the office. Being the London we know and love, it's a cold, grey morning. You're chilled to the bone and half asleep. You can barely face the day ahead. You need that cup of coffee.

- No choice, so you invariably enter a basic, undecorated, local sandwich bar. This is nirvana if your idea of calm and relaxation combines a healthy dose of formica, a lot of linoleum, some residual grease stains, and a smattering of grime.

- You stand in a long queues and watch staff go about their work. That's making sandwiches, by the way!

- While queuing you stare at an exhibit that even an avantgarde modern artist couldn't come up with. Rows and rows of plastic tubs filled with congealed crab mayo, congealed tuna mayo, congealed egg mayo and ashen slices of what once passed (a long, long time ago) for roast beef, the sort which had seen better days in the eighties. None of the above have even been turned over from the day before to hide the glutinous crusts that have formed on their surfaces. Not a nice sight at 8.00 a.m.

- The sandwich maker who is taking your money with his bare hands (note hygiene, or the lack of it!) makes you a quick cappuccino on the side. You can't decide whether you're more worried that he hasn't washed his hands because he might have been to the bathroom, or because he's touched the food that I've described above! You think you could catch something either way!

- You get your hot drink (which I am loath to call coffee) in a polystyrene cup that goes floppy in your hand. As for the lid, well, it's a flat plastic thing with a nasty little hole in it that fits about as well as shoes that are two sizes too small, meaning that if you want to walk with your coffee, burned hands are part of the experience.

- In short, morning coffee in London is not a great deal of fun, unless you like feeling hassled, grubby and unmotivated. By the time you get to work, you hate the day already.

This is what our new style coffee bar will provide:

- You leave same stifling tube station.

- But you enter a place distinctly designed and branded to enhance your coffee experience – a comfortable, warm environment able to accommodate a big volume of traffic yet to be inviting and accommodating at the same time.

- Although you are queuing you can listen to gentle, soothing music and view the delicious range of tempting coffee compliments while you do so.

- You are served by uniformed, highly trained 'baristas' who make your coffee to order and to your individual requirements with four types of milk, strength, decaf, half-caf, iced, etc.

- You take away your coffee in a specially designed and branded sturdy cup with a domed lid which doesn't steal foam off your cappuccino. Plus, you have four choices of toppings to round things off.

Who wouldn't go for it? Surely everyone would love it? In the US they've taken a basic commodity and made it into pure luxury — but not any luxury — a luxury that's part of your daily commute. Happiness, in other words, at the most stressful time of the day.
Thinking of possible strap lines:
It's a break from the daily grind.
It's like upgrading your day!
It's an affordable luxury.
Treat yourself.

It's all so exciting: It feels so right!

Sahar

We've now told you our story. You can see that our idea
- Wasn't novel or original or revolutionary.
- We were our own first customers.
- We saw the gap in the market.
- We didn't have any particular skills or industry experience.

We had found the light bulb. It was all gut-instinct stuff at this stage, but that is all the light bulb stage is about. Our idea felt right on the first night we talked about it, and the next morning it still felt right. At the end of the next day after a bit of investigation it felt even better. We knew that a bona fide light bulb had been turned on.

"Everything that is, ever was or ever will be once started as an idea in someone's mind." - WALLY AMOS

Now what?

CHAPTER THREE:
MARKET RESEARCH
TURNING THE IDEA INTO A BUSINESS

So you've got a great idea for starting a business and you feel confident in your vision. The reality, however, is that you're no more than .01% of the way down the road to entrepreneurship. Gut instinct has got you on the road, but conviction is what you will now need to employ to follow it successfully.

Almost all of us, at some stage in our lives, have dreamed of starting our own business but very few of us are able to turn the dream into a concrete reality. The fundamental reason for this is that progress almost inevitably stalls at the 'idea stage', that point where a business light bulb has to leave the comfort of the imagination and enter into the real world.

"If everyone who has talked about starting a business actually went out and did it, the whole nation would be self-employed. But most people would rather fantasize about it than do it."
- MARK McCORMACK, author of *What they don't teach you at Harvard Business School*

Law 16: An idea not acted upon is worthless

Since we started Coffee Republic, countless people have told us that they had the same idea that we did, in a great many cases even before us. They, too, had been to the United States and had indulged in the coffee bar experience that so captured our own imaginations. On their return to England, they had pondered the idea of opening a similar concept in the UK. A great many of these people were probably better equipped (from the perspective of skills and experience) to pursue the idea than we were. Yet they didn't do it.

"A new idea is delicate. It can be killed by a sneer or a yawn: It can be stabbed to death by a joke or worried to death by a frown on the wrong person's brow."

- CHARLES BROWDER

The thing that separates entrepreneurs is really very simple. While others dream, entrepreneurs see a good idea through to fruition. Whereas for most people an idea is cast aside after a couple of investigatory phone calls and perhaps a few discouraging comments from the so-called 'experts', entrepreneurs don't quit, even when all they have to go on is gut instinct. They keep working hard to realise their dreams. The entrepreneurial mind thinks like this: "I don't have any experience, or special skills, I don't have the money. I have no idea how I'm going to do it. But I'm still going to do it."

Almost inevitably, if you're reading this book, you'll have found yourself in a position similar to the one described above at some time in the past. Why didn't you move forward? Did you doubt your own ability? When it came to the crunch, did you feel that your idea wasn't quite viable enough? Or did you imagine that someone better suited would beat you to the punch? Perhaps your friends and acquaintances, on the other hand, convinced you that you weren't quite up to the task of starting a business. Sahar remembers a friend who tried to dissuade her from going ahead with Coffee Republic. He said "Do you have any idea what bearing the responsibility for monthly employee pay cheques is really like?" Sahar didn't know, but she went for it anyway. That attitude represents the difference between commitment and procrastination. Entrepreneurs commit; others fail to get the job done.

Law 17: Entrepreneurs do not procrastinate

They don't approach their business idea by asking "Do my chances of failure outweigh my chances of success?" just as Sahar didn't when her friend questioned her. Instead, entrepreneurs say "I am committed to this idea. I appreciate that it may only be half-baked and semi-coherent for now, but I AM going to do it. The only question is 'how', not 'if'"

While procrastination is the thief of ideas, the secret ingredient to overcoming it is very simple: commitment. But where do you find commitment, when you have nothing more than an abstract idea – even a great one – to keep you going? How can you find enough commitment to keep working on something on which you've spent no more than a day developing? The good news is that you don't just go out and 'get commitment'.

Law 18: Commitment is generated by working on your idea

That's right! Commitment is not a mysterious formula that some of us can generate and others can't. Commitment is something each of us can build within ourselves as we actually begin working on our idea. Anyone can find commitment. It doesn't simply come hand-in-hand with an idea, but rather it is the by-product of not procrastinating and, instead, actually working on the idea. If you leave an idea to languish on the mantelpiece, you will never be committed to it, but if you do something about your idea then your commitment will grow on a daily basis in equal proportion to the effort that you put into it.

In other words if you have an idea, start working on it immediately. You may find that your level of commitment is weak at the start, but as soon as you dip your toes in the water that will change. You will start to learn whether or not you're on the right track and, as the information you're looking for starts to come in, your commitment will either wither or grow exponentially depending on what you learn. If it withers, don't worry! You've still acted in an entrepreneurial way because you have not allowed yourself to be discouraged from 'going for it'. Not every idea is right, and others will soon come your way. If you're lucky, and you find yourself believing that you're on the right path, then you will experience a dramatic inner shift. Your commitment will gradually escalate and become a burning determination. Then absolutely nothing will be able to stop you from reaching your goal!

Our Story – how we found commitment.

To find out the answer, we'll now take you back to the Thai restaurant on the King's Road that we mentioned a little earlier. That was a critical evening, even a defining moment in our lives, because the key to Coffee Republic was very simply that we didn't leave our idea hanging in space between us on the table that night.

After we'd talked about our idea over dinner, we didn't go home thinking "we'll come back to this later" or "we'll do some passive investigating over the coming weeks and see what happens". Instead, Sahar decided to check out the coffee market for herself. Was she right about the lack of a good coffee experience in London? She set out to convince herself by finding the answers.

The next morning, with the well of enthusiasm still full from the conversation of the previous evening, Sahar left her flat bound for the nearest underground station intent on taking the first concrete steps on the road to turning the coffee bar idea into a reality. The precise purpose of Sahar's expedition was to prove that a gap in the market existed, but that wasn't really the crucial point about the effect of that critical morning's work.

> **THE KEY WAS THIS: WE ACTED.**

With no delay whatsoever, we took our idea one step further and brought it out into the real world. By acting on an idea, the idea ceases to exist only in the imagination and becomes instead the physical embryo of the business that is ultimately created.

The idea starts in a state of inertia and you need to get it into motion. It's all about momentum, really. Momentum builds as a result of each step you take forward, no matter how small. Lots of small steps equal serious momentum, whereas if you do nothing and fail to take any concrete steps at all, your business idea will never see the light of day.

In just over twelve hours, from the restaurant conversation to Sahar's circuitous journey around London, our idea had taken physical steps and we had momentum on our side. In no time at all, therefore, we had exponentially increased our chances of bringing our idea into the world of reality. We had already embarked on the ladder of commitment.

Have you ever had this sort of conversation?

YOU: *"I have a great idea for a business."*

FRIEND: *"That sounds great. But a word of caution…"*

ANOTHER FRIEND: *"Yes, I tried something like that once. It will never work. It didn't for me…"*

YET ANOTHER FRIEND: *"Well, good idea, but let me play the devil's advocate…"*

YOU: *"Mmmmm, well, it did seem like a good idea, though I can see that I ought to have reservations."*

THE FIRST FRIEND: *"No, you go ahead. But never forget that it won't be easy and you almost certainly won't succeed."*

YOU: *"Oh well, it was just an idea. Let's talk about something else."*

Sounds familiar, doesn't it?

When you are committed, you don't let any of that bother you because you have a deep passion and certainty which will carry you through the minefield of obstacles, rejections and doubts that you will face. That's not to say that you won't have doubts, fears and insecurities about your venture. It's just that you're not going to let them stop you. You'll be working in spite of all the doubts and naysayers so you will eventually move beyond them. One day when you are immersed in the work, you will realize that all the doubts and insecurities are somewhere in the background or have vanished altogether.

> **SO THE BEST ADVICE IS: START WORKING IMMEDIATELY!**

Where do you begin?
You've got your idea and you've perhaps taken a first physical step towards achieving your goal (in our case, that was Sahar's journey on the Circle Line), but now you need something more. The initial action has committed you to the cause, but you're still at the stage where you recognise that you're some distance away from your ultimate destination. So what happens now? How do you take another step up the commitment ladder?

Your next step is Market Research.

Law 19: Market research is nothing more than a massive fact-finding mission

It really is that simple. So far you've listened to your own inner voice. This is the stage where you start listening to others. It's about backing up your gut feel with real facts and figures so that you are convinced about your idea. Your conviction has to be so strong that you can persuade others about your idea.

The market research bottom-line commandment is simple: find out as much as you can from as many sources as possible about your business. Live it, sleep it, and breathe it. Here are a few helpful lessons that we learned at this stage.

Law 20: Follow the Zulu Principle

Coined by the 1970s takeover guru Jim Slater, this rule (named for his wife's knowledge of the African tribe) asserts that anyone can become an expert about anything if they focus on it completely. Slater's wife became an expert on Zulus with no prior knowledge of them until she read a single magazine article.

We became Zulus about the coffee business. We decided that we would learn, as simple as it sounds, everything and anything there was to know about coffee and the business of coffee. It didn't matter that one of us was a lawyer and one of us was an investment banker. We wanted to immerse ourselves in the world of coffee and become experts in that field as quickly as we possibly could.

What we did to achieve this sounds incredibly simple, but it is all that market research really is. We read about coffee wherever we could find that anyone had written something. We talked about coffee at every opportunity, between ourselves and with anyone interested enough to share their opinions with us. We drank coffee wherever and whenever we could. Every time we came across something abstract (such as a magazine article about general business issues, or a vacant retail site, or a advertisement for retail staff), we personalised it in our own minds and sought to understand how it impacted or affected us. As a result, we noticed mundane and trivial things we had never seen before.

Everything around us became a part of the opportunity that stretched out before our idea. In a shorter time than you might imagine, we probably knew more about coffee than many who had been in the business for years. We were true Zulus of the coffee world!

Law 21: When it comes to market research, do it yourself!

As we said earlier, market research is about listening to others and your own ears need to do the listening, not someone else's. There is simply no substitute for the motivation, determination and thoroughness that you'll bring to the job. A hired researcher will not have the motivation to challenge and absorb information like you will. A slick research agency might give you a glossy report packed with facts and figures, but do the work yourself and you'll know the story behind them too.

Besides, while you're doing your research you'll have all sorts of unexpected moments of real inspiration. You'll spot the small things a dispassionate professional might miss, but which will allow you to develop and embellish your idea still further. In other words, keep your idea firmly within reach and get your hands dirty; it will pay off. Even when you're not actively working, you'll find that you're passively researching your idea.

Law 22: Inspiration is all around you

The more you physically immerse yourself in your idea, the more inspired moments to which you'll be exposed. Ideas will just come to you. The simple process of learning about your business will bring things to your attention that you will probably never have seen before.

Funnily enough, the pursuit of hard facts (your market research) will actually result in your creative side being given a boost. As you mull over what you're learning and toss in random thoughts of your own, you'll create a fertile ground in which to cultivate new ideas. That combination of facts and figures along with inspired thinking will serve to increase the momentum that you've already started to build, and you'll really begin to see your dream taking shape in your mind.

WHAT DO YOU RESEARCH?

There are four main areas surrounding your idea, about which you need to learn. These are:

- **The Market:** In other words, study the industry you will be operating in and how your business will fit in with care. What is the market size (in other words the size of the opportunity) you're facing? What are the future, the past and the present trends? Who are the main players in your industry? Who owns what? What are the issues affecting the industry? What will be your likely position? What market share do you hope to achieve?

- **Customers:** Who are your customers? Do they have common characteristics? What are their buying habits? Why do they buy, then do they buy (at work, at home, on holiday) and how often (once a year or daily)? What do they pay for (convenience, quality, experience)? What prices are they willing to pay and, perhaps, do they have needs, conscious or unconscious, which are not presently being met by the existing market? If they do, how will you be able to meet them? Furthermore, is there something unique that you can offer to win these customers over – is there any added benefit you can offer them?

- **Competition:** Who are your competitors? What is their market share, and what is their offer (pricing, positioning, etc.)? How well are they performing? How can you differentiate your business from theirs? How will you price your product? Who will be your competitors in future?

- **Suppliers:** Who are they? What do they supply? Who do they supply? What are their prices? Do they supply what you need?

HOW DO YOU ACTUALLY DO THE RESEARCH?

You need to know anything and everything you can find out about your potential business, so your research is actually an immersion course in a particular subject. The danger here is that when everything is fair game, you can easily lose a sense of structure and thus lose sight of your objectives. We found that it was important to set about market research in an organised way. We did the following, which proved useful for us.

Desk research (it's time for homework)

This is straightforward and seemingly unexciting, but it is in many ways a fantastic starting point for your journey. It enables you give yourself a foundation of hard knowledge before hitting the streets for more personal investigations. You can also gather the statistics and hard facts that you'll need. Desk research has a simple goal: you want to get your hands on every thing that has ever been published about your business. If there is something to know, you want to know it.

This sounds like homework – but it's much more fun; you'll be so hungry for the information.

Your first port of call should be your local business library. If you are in London, the City Business Library is an invaluable business information source. They have great staff that can help you find all the information you need. The library has a collection of:

- Directories
- Market reports
(which would cost thousands if you were to buy them yourself)
- Periodicals
- Newspapers
- Annual reports and other information on companies
- Government information
- Trade information and trade press publications

You should also contact your relevant trade association. A great many of these have their own reference libraries, containing publications of specific interest that you can often access at no cost.

You can sometimes find trade magazines at public libraries but if not, it is worth discovering which titles cover your proposed field and subscribing to them where possible. Reading these publications will keep you abreast of what is going on in the business. At the back in the advertising section you often get a good list of the suppliers you need.

Organise a cuttings file. We suggest keeping a scrapbook of any newspaper cuttings that appear that might be relevant to the business you wish to start. These may be specific to your field of business, or more generally related to economic conditions or issues related to starting a business.

Although we did not have Internet access at time of our research, it is an invaluable source of information now, especially if you've picked up the leads you need from your library homework.

Hit the road!
This will be your most effective research – making phone calls, meeting people, visiting competitors, and seeing other retail concepts. In fact, anything that will bring you face-to-face with an aspect of your idea. You will be amazed by how much you can learn just by pursuing the obvious, how a brief chat, a cursory phone call or a quick meeting can lead to a nugget of information that you will find invaluable later on.

Where do you start? Well, the Yellow Pages are a great place. Telephone ten suppliers, ten competitors if you're in retail, ten surveyors and ten shop fitters. You'll know which questions you want to ask.

Then visit your competitors. Visit other businesses that inspire you and see what you can learn. Go to locations that you think might be right for your idea. When you're on the road, the physical shape of your business will become as clear as the facts and figures you learned at your desk.

We will share with you the market research rules we learned (sometimes the hard way) so, with benefit of hindsight, you won't make the mistakes we did!

Law 23: Do NOT give the game away. Be discreet

Write this one in big red letters and never forget it! When you're full of enthusiasm and chatting away on a subject near and dear to you, the easiest thing in the world is to reveal more of your plans than you really should.

Instead, play your cards close to your chest. Be vague about your idea and be cautious rather than over-the-top in your enthusiasm.

However, also bear in mind that you should never lie. You will be speaking to people with whom, in some cases, you might be building long-term relationships so it is important not to mislead them entirely. You need to strike a balance between being positive and not giving away your best ideas.

When we worked on our idea, we quickly learned that the coffee industry was packed with rumours about the US coffee craze. We simply tried to get as much information as possible without giving the game away.

Law 24: Call as many people as you can bear to – there's safety in numbers

Another area in which you need to be persistent is your phone calling. A lot of people won't be able to, or won't want to, talk to you and it's important that your chin doesn't drop when a string of 'rejections' comes in. Always bear in mind that after five negative phone calls, the sixth may yield an invaluable source of inside information and, in any case, our experience demonstrates that the majority of people that you speak to will give you a surprising amount of useful advice.

Also, remember that one phone call leads to another. Those who speak freely with you are often willing to open their address books and point you in other, equally useful, directions.

Law 25: Don't be selective. Go to everything

As you start introducing yourself to the market, and this is particularly true of suppliers, you will receive invitations to visit people. After a while, the appeal of yet another trudge to yet another salesman's office might have lost its charm but we strongly advise: don't say "no". You never know what you'll learn, and you never know what you'll be offered unless you take the initiative and go.

In our case, one of the suppliers we visited had an introductory training course on coffee making that we were able to attend for free. There we learned many of the tricks of the trade, and we met others who were opening coffee shops not dissimilar in concept to ours. The trading of information that took place between us was invaluable.

If you think all this sounds exciting, interesting and straight-forward, be warned that it's at this point that being an entrepreneur can start to put a strain on your health! Well, that's certainly true if you're going into a caffeine-related business. One day, after our nth visit to a supplier and after a formal tasting of each of their fourteen blends of espresso, for fear of heart failure we suddenly had to pull in to a service station on the M4 and polish off two Mars bars each in rapid succession simply to absorb the overdose of caffeine!

Anyway, we spent an enormous amount of invaluable time visiting coffee bars, cafes, and other food-related concepts. If any literature was available, we took it home and studied it. In very short order, we became experts on what was happening on the coffee scene, and if we learned about anything new, we made sure we were the first to visit.

Whilst we were doing our market research, Sahar also made an extremely useful diversion. She returned to New York to really investigate every facet of the original source of our idea, this time in as much depth as possible. This trip we look on as our reconnaissance mission.

After a late night flight the preceding day, Sahar got up at 5.00 a.m. on her first morning back in the city, donned her Timberlands, and set out on her coffee exploration quest. By 10.30 a.m. she was ten skinny lattes and twenty-five muffins the worse for wear, so you can only imagine how she felt when the reconnaissance mission ended three days later. The only degree of relief available was provided by the walks between coffee bars, without which she'd have been occupying two seats rather than one on the return flight.

Lest you're worried that Sahar's research trip to New York was actually little more than a thinly veiled excuse to eat a lot (and we do mean a lot), let us assure you that wasn't the case. She gathered what became an indispensable visual album of the concept we sought to emulate. Armed with disposable cameras and deploying considerable sleight of hand, she snapped away at food counters, layouts, condiment stations and employee uniforms as she munched away at muffins, brownies and doughnuts.

Occasionally she was caught red-handed and faced the moderate humiliation of ejection from the premises. One manager actually chased her out of the store. So, ever creative, Sahar then took to employing friends to photograph her on her 'wonderful trip to New York', resulting in a post-modern portfolio of coffee shop abstracts displaying images such as a row of espresso machines with the lobe of Sahar's ear just visible in the top corner. By the way, when anyone now walks into Coffee Republic with a camera well, just don't. We know what you're up to!

Law 26: Become a regular of the competition

Before your own idea becomes a reality, your competitors are the best way to learn about the challenges that you will face.

By the time we opened our first store, we probably knew the competition almost as well as we knew our own idea. Furthermore, we adapted our lifestyles to imitate those of our typical customer. So every morning we went to what we thought were the best of the old-style coffee bars in search of a daily cup, and this inspired us to remain excited as well as to continually visualise what we could offer.

It may seem unfair, but it's the best way of getting to know your future business and once you're in business, others will do it to you. So it is fair game!

By constantly being exposed to our chosen future environment in this way, the momentum we had already built up was both maintained and intensified. Even when we weren't actively working on our idea, we were passively absorbing a steady diet of information about the coffee business.

"check everyone who is our competitor. And don't look bad. Look for the good. If you get one good idea, then one more than you went into the store with and we must incorporate it into our company."

Advice from SAM WALTON of Wal-Mart to his employees

Law 27: Formal customer surveys are OUT!

You want to think outside the box. Do not spend thousands of pounds with an agency that asks, on your behalf, a select group of prospective customers about their likely behaviour in a certain situation. Spending money this way is just not worth it. Save the cash, and use what you save to do a better job of actually developing your product.

"If I had asked customers what they wanted they would have said a faster horse." - HENRY FORD

The reason for this is that if you ask customers what they want, you will get constrained by their current needs. Your role as an entrepreneur is to serve needs they haven't yet articulated but would love to have satisfied. You're anticipating and serving a future need.

If you want proof of this, there's a famous Henry Ford quote that puts our argument perfectly. He was right. His customers would not have been able to articulate a preference for something with which they were unfamiliar. How could coffee drinkers in London know what they thought of US-style coffee bars when the majority of them had never experienced one?

Besides, being unconventional and having the courage of your convictions is part of what makes a successful entrepreneur. Don't forget that you are a pioneer.

Don't allow yourself to be locked within the boundaries of the existing status quo. As long as you've studied current habits and are able to offer something better than the competition in a price range your customers can afford, then go for it!

"Marketing is giving people things they never knew they wanted." - YVES SAINT LAURENT

Our Story – what did we do?

ere are a couple of faxes between us, starting on the morning after that very first night (when our idea was born at the Thai Restaurant on the King's Road) and ending some time later when the road to reality had really taken shape. We think what stands out is the simplicity of what was involved and what we did: of course we were thorough and dedicated, but as you'll see that nothing which follows is rocket science. That is why we are so confident that anyone can do it!

FACSIMILE (FROM BOBBY)

Sahar,

These are the issues we need to focus on at this 'market research' stage:

1. You should see the point of the next few weeks as an exercise in market immersion.
   Your primary goal is to get the 'pulse of the coffee market'.

2. You need to start first with 'desk research', which I suggest you do by: Finding a business library and going through news clippings, coffee company annual reports, research analyst reports and records of the latest US trends. Really research in detail the state of the coffee market both here and in US.
   If you can, find out if any of the 'big boys' (large food companies) are planning coffee bars in the UK?

3. While you're researching as above, always keep thinking about our message. Everything you discover you should look at with that in mind. Remember, it should be simple, crisp, and clear.

   Also, find out who are our competitors and why are we will be different from them? Visualise our store — the atmosphere, the focus on quality, and how we'll be different from the crap presently on the market.

4. Your market research should give a ballpark hint on retail prices, property prices and our cost of goods (coffee). Can you put together a crude profit and loss spreadsheet and see how much coffee we need to sell to break even?

Don't let this worry you. It's not as difficult as it sounds. I have to say that we will never get a precise answer no matter how much we crunch numbers. At the end of the day it comes down to our judgment of whether we can achieve breakeven sales. My gut instinct is to start out small in every sense (i.e. minimum square footage needed that would still differentiate us and give our message clearly. If you have huge windows you might need a lot less space).

Sahar, don't worry about financing now. Focus on concept and if the concept is good we will somehow come up with the dosh! We basically have one FULL YEAR (1995) to establish and create a brand name!! Not much time at all!!

Xx

B

FACSIMILE (FROM SAHAR)

Methods of research

I think I've done the bulk of my market research. My methods of research have been:

- Extensive press cutting research at City Business Library on coffee, coffee shops and competition (there is actually a magazine called Café Ole with all gossip on new coffee bars).
- Reading up-to-date marketing reports (I found Mintel has the best on fast food industry) held at City business

Library (too expensive to buy and illegal to photocopy!)
- Visited library of International Coffee Organisation (imagine a library ALL about coffee) — really good press cuttings.
- Prospectuses of big US and UK food chains.
- Telephoning competitors and asking for info...I've got a mini map of London with all our competitors marked on it.
- I've called most of the coffee and coffee machine suppliers. Totally incognito, of course.

This is what I've learned:

MARKET

- Coffee is the world's second largest traded commodity after oil.
- Tea has always been the favourite national beverage in the UK (3.9 cups per person per day). It used to be seven times bigger than coffee but the gap between tea and coffee is slowly reducing.
- UK has one of lowest per capita consumption of coffee in Europe. At one time UK consumed 2 kilos of coffee per capita while it was 5 kilos in France and 6 kilos in Germany. Scandinavian countries consume around 14 kilos per capita.
- UK is Europe's only country with a huge preference for instant. 90% of the coffee drunk in UK is instant, compared to France where 10% only is instant.
- There is a real upward trend in coffee consumption making it the most buoyant segment in the grocery market. 63% of the real coffee consumed in UK is drunk outside the home. So there is tremendous potential for growth in the UK.
- The sandwich market is booming. It is going through what we believe the coffee bar market will soon be going through. Basically the market is innovating and moving towards higher quality with grocery multiples and Pret A Manger challenging the dominance of old-style sandwich bars.
- More general consumer trend is demand for convenience products because changes in lifestyle and erosion of family mealtimes have led to an increase in snacking and eating between meals.

COFFEE

- I've learnt all about coffee — there's a fascinating story about Kaldi, by the way. Remind me to tell you sometime!

- Spoken to 10 coffee suppliers
  (of course I didn't tell them about our real plans.
  I pretended to be opening normal sandwich bar!) – got
  good idea on costs and gross margin on cappuccino –
  you'd be impressed!
- Spoken to main coffee machine suppliers and I have
  obtained brochures and prices.
- Asked around and got general idea of numbers of cups
  sold.
  Sandwich bars sell 1000s of cappuccinos a day – can you
  believe it?
- Complied list of competitors prices.
- I even called Customs And Excise about import duty if we
  import equipment from USA.

THE SITE

My first lead was my university friend Philip, now a
successful chartered surveyor. He explained whole process
to me. We need to appoint a chartered surveyor who will a
find site for us and generally advise us on everything,
which is great as I was worried about our lack of ANY
knowledge in this area.

- Thus, I've contacted some key surveyors – got their
  names off the boards on retail sites – they gave me
  ballpark rent and rate figures.
- Obtained general idea of IDEAL locations for us based
  on visiting areas personally to check out competition
  and foot traffic. I'm also using my own previous
  instinct and experience.
- The main problem they all say is that institutional
  landlords will not give start-ups like us a lease
  without a personal guarantee. This will be our biggest
  problem. Red flag this area!!
- Got an idea about planning permission.
- Sussed out environmental health. No problems foreseen,
  just register with them and involve them in shop –
  fitting plans.

To Do: As regards finding cheap, good, imaginative
locations, it seems the only person who will bother to
look is me. Surveyors aren't giving me time of day. They
just send me their leaflets for dud sites. I need to drive
around the city myself and look at vacant properties.
Once I find a good empty shop then I'll contact a surveyor
who can approach a landlord on my behalf.

To Do: The cheapest way to get numbers on foot traffic is to do it myself – I have just bought 'counter' from Ryman and click number of people that pass a site at key rush hours.

It seems to me that until we establish a brand we should stay away from British Rail and Heathrow. Those markets are well looked after by the big guys. They told me that not only do they have no vacancies but they only accept brand names anyway!

My favourite locations:
Moorgate
Sloane Square
Fleet Street/Holborn

OVERHEADS

I've got a general idea now on typical overheads. Called up utilities and their business divisions were really helpful. They give you an estimate if you are a coffee bar of certain size of how much your utilities bill will be.

EMPLOYEES

No clue about how many employees we need but I know that we can't have one serving 400 cups a day. That would be impossible, especially if we get peaks. Or is it possible? Who can we ask? Maybe I'll ask a coffee supplier.

The most important thing I have discovered is the huge importance of well-trained and highly-motivated employees. I've found a coffee supplier that has 2 training days a month and we can send our employees there for free. Another supplier told me they are all paid on an hourly basis, so fewer legal formalities for us.

To Do: Find out how many employees we need? Where I can find employees that are totally different to the ones you see in Italian sandwich bars? Where do I buy employee uniforms (thinking T-shirt, baseball cap and apron, all with logos)?

SHOP FITTING

I really have no clue here. I have only got a ballpark estimate from shop fitters that I found in the Yellow Pages. Maybe it will get clearer once we find a site. Can we get copy of a design from NY architects? Is that a ridiculous idea?

FOOD

I've done some asking around. But none of them seem to offer the quality we want. Nobody does fat-free muffins – they think I'm mad. What about sandwiches? In NY they sell them but is that because coffee doesn't make money? Then again, let's not sell sandwiches, as we are not a restaurant.

To Do: Might have to commission baker to bake just for us to get the quality we need. I will buy a fat-free recipe book from NY.

Sales other than COFFEE

TO DO: I need someone to tell me whether I need to sell other drinks than coffee. My own instinct is we should sell OJ, tea, and water. If two people go out to buy breakfast together and one is not a coffee drinker, they wouldn't want to stand in two queues, so coffee drinker will sacrifice on quality and buy his coffee where they also sell tea. Also, let's not forget this is still a nation of tea drinkers!!

COMPETITION

Although there is no one at the moment in London with our concept, I hear that two other companies are opening and there is a lot of talk about it in the market. Starbucks have been over to look, but they have their hands full with expanding in the US.

To Do: What if new style coffee bars start sprouting around London before we manage to open? What if big US player or someone with significant economic power opens round the corner from us? My answer is we have to open ASAP to establish market presence and loyalty before everyone else. If someone opens we should then be able to compete with them on the basis of our strong image and brand loyalty which would by then have been established.

FINANCIALS

Estimate number of visitors. I got figures from London transport – 26,963 people walk out of Moorgate tube station and if we are prominently located and lure 10% of them, that's 2600 people!!! If Marks & Spencers sold 3.5m sandwiches last year from Moorgate at a rate of 13500 a day there must be a volume of 800 people going into that store! All the suppliers I spoke to say we should sell a MINIMUM 400-500 cups per day!

Anyway my pavement count should help us on these.
S

Law 28: The 80:20 Rule

Once you've done the research, however, we'll bet that like us one question will still remain gnawing away at the forefront of your mind. Before you totally, utterly commit to your idea, quit your job, and jump in head-first you will want to know:

HOW CAN I BE ONE HUNDRED PERCENT SURE THAT MY IDEA WILL WORK?

We can answer that question for you: YOU CAN'T. There will always be many unanswered questions.

We advocate the 80/20 rule: As long as you have 80% of the issues covered, you can afford to leave the 20% unanswered. Your gut instinct will help you figure out the other 20% you need to know as you go along.

When we got to the end of our research stage, we still had a few unanswered questions. The biggest one was pretty important, too...

WHAT DO I CALL THE BUSINESS?

Every entrepreneur faces the obvious and inevitable question: What am I going to call my business? In retail, where brand is paramount, this decision is even more important. We didn't actually come up with the name Coffee Republic until March 1995, and it took us four months to find it. That wasn't a problem though, as time devoted to getting the name right is time well spent indeed.

With that in mind, here are some thoughts born of our experience of finding a name. We think that a name should really encapsulate all the practical and emotional feelings about your business. It should give your customers an indication of the benefits you offer them on both a practical and an emotional level.

"While your strategy might be the primary reason for your success, a good name tends to protect your company from competitive encroachments into your territory. A bad name, on the other hand, is a millstone around your neck." - AL RIES, the author of Focus

---

HOW TO FIND A NAME

Perhaps a good way to go about finding a name is to start by jotting down a few notes in list form. Start with the practical benefits your product will supply:

- Is it cheaper?
- Is it better?
- Is it more convenient?
- Does it offer a new special benefit?

Then write out the emotional benefit a customer should associate with you when they hear your name:

- Better experience.
- Better product.
- Value for money.
- Reliability. Coolness.

Your business name plays a very important role, especially at the beginning before you have established a dialogue and reputation with your customers. It should give a feel for what your offer will be like and it must capture the 'character' of your business.

We just couldn't figure out a name to do justice to the concept we were visualizing. It was such a key point and yet we had no solution. We struggled with a lot of names that never felt right. Itwas a frustrating period. Turn over and you will find a page from our scrapbook, notes we made at the time that bears out what we went through!

When all was done and dusted, the name we came up with was Java Express. We actually wrote our business plan and raised money as Java Express. But guess what? In our hearts, we knew all along that Java Express was not right.

The name should:

- Immediately tell the customer what we're about, i.e. coffee!
- Encapsulate our dedication to the perfect coffee experience.
- Give the feeling that you've entered a branded world where all is consistent.
- Give customers a feel for the experience 'affordable luxury'.
- Relay the fact that's its an exciting new concept, i.e. our wide choice.
- Stand out on the high street and be different from trad sandwich bars.
- Be catchy so it grabs attention.
- Be a name you can use as part of your daily life.
- Be cool and trendy but not too élite and niche.
- Be for ANYONE who wants a great coffee!

HOW TO FIND THE 'AHA!' NAME

1. Keep your name search in mind throughout the research stage, when you are at your most creative. As you are out and about at this time, you will be passively thinking about it, and you may be surprised when a good idea suddenly appears.

2. Brainstorm with friends. Our friends suggested wacky names like 'Che Guevara Coffee' and 'Has Bean'. You won't always get gems of advice but it's never a waste of time.

3. Look through the yellow pages at other businesses' names. You won't be able to copy any of those, but you'll get some broad ideas and also learn what not to do.

4. Look through US phone directories as well (especially from lesser-known States). Incidentally, you will be able to copy these.

5. Browse through lifestyle/fashion magazines. You can find great food for thought and sometimes a headline or word combination can really jump out at you.

6. Brainstorm with yourself and a pad of paper. Write down and sketch everything that comes to your mind for half an hour every day. Just start by sketching anything you can visualise, however crazy it seems!

7. Once you've found the 'aha!' name, sleep on it, try it out on people and check their reaction. If its still OK in the light of day - then you've got yourself a name!

As we looked for a name, there was one source of pressure. We needed to register a limited company and we wanted to register it with the right name at the outset. We went back to the City Business Library and we remember both going through telephone directories of various places in the US like Minnesota and Seattle to get inspiration. We invited a group of friends around and brainstormed. In short, we did everything we've suggested that you try…and no luck! Finally, one day we were stuck in traffic outside South Kensington tube station. We both remember the exact moment:

"Bobby, the thing about the name is it should show customers that it's all about coffee. It's like walking into coffee country, where everything is about your coffee experience. Coffee world…COFFEE REPUBLIC…"

Sahar immediately looked back at Bobby knowing she had hit the bull's-eye. He immediately shouted in response: "That's it!" It was the 'aha!' moment. Instinctively and instantly we both knew that Coffee Republic captured everything about the soul of the business we visualized. We got home and called three friends immediately, all of whom confirmed our certainty that the name was right. In fact it was spot on; with the benefit of hindsight it definitely was the right name. Five years later it was listed in the Financial Times as one of the five brands that represent New Britain.

And that, on the subject of research, is it! In truth, your research stage will never officially end because there's always more to learn about your business. At some point, you simply have to leap.

"Leap and the net will appear!" - JULIA CAMERON

CHAPTER FOUR:
WRITING THE BUSINESS PLAN
TURNING THE IDEA INTO A BUSINESS

As you come to the end of your research and develop more and more conviction for your idea, you will start to ask yourself "how do I actually turn this idea into a business?" You have arrived at the point where you need to sit down and write a business plan.

This is the time when you'll move from the world of information gathering and immersion in your idea to the deliberate, systematic, step-by-step planning of the process by which you'll take your great (but abstract) idea into becoming a living, breathing, operating business.

It's time to add organisation to the enthusiasm that has until now been enough to get you by.

DO YOU HAVE TO DO A BUSINESS PLAN?

Yes. Not to do so would be like building a house without a blueprint.

It's true that Bill Gates and Paul Allen didn't write a business plan for Microsoft's first product, but then again they didn't do any market research either. They are the exception rather than the rule. Two out of three small business start without a business plan and the same percentage of them fail within five years. That is not accidental.

Why is having a business plan not optional?

Law 29: It's your recipe for success

The words 'business plan' send the less business-minded among us running for shelter because of the intimidating and technical aspects the words bring to mind. Never fear, however. We are not talking about rocket science. Business plans are simply a formal list of your objectives and a road map which illustrates how you plan to achieve them with a budget for doing so attached.

If it still sounds daunting, look at it this way. If you're going on holiday, you don't wake up one morning and say "Right then, I'm off for two weeks. Where shall I go?" What you do (and you've done it before) is three months or so in advance of your time off, you get organised. You think about where you'll go, you think about what it will cost, you work out how much money you have to spend, you make reservations and so on. So when the big day arrives, you're ready to get out of bed and set off.

If you've ever organised and gone on a holiday, you've already more or less written a business plan. In fact, if you've ever run any event that required a combination of forward planning and budgeting (holding a party would be another example), then you already have business planning experience to draw on. A business plan is nothing more than a recipe for your business.

Law 30: It's a structured brain dump,
and brain dumps need structure

Up until now, you have built momentum from a combination of commitment, enthusiasm and research. You'll be riding on the crest of a wave of observations, facts, details and random thoughts that will most likely be scattered all around your mind. You probably know everything there is to know about your proposed business, but that knowledge will have very little shape or form. Everything you've done to date, in other words, needs to be organised before it becomes useful. The business plan is the filing system you impose upon your idea.

Filing systems, like business plans, do not sound exciting but whether at home or in the office, if you've ever needed to find something urgently and had no idea where it is, then you already know how important they are. They are what turns information alone into information that can be used.

In your business plan, you will take all the random ideas and information you have amassed and commit it to paper. By writing everything out, your ideas become clearer and the business takes on a real shape. Furthermore, you'll come across and be forced to address all the things that you've forgotten or overlooked.

"If you can't write it, you don't know it."

It's best to write your business plan both during and straight after the research stage because it's at this time that you will be at your most creative and informed regarding your idea and the market. You will be fresh and excited about things so you will write down all your thoughts and plans without forgetting anything, which might happen if you don't put things on paper until a later date. Another benefit is that as time passes on you will find yourself getting more and more bogged down in the day-to-day details of starting your business. It is then that you will relish referring back to the business plan just to remind yourself why you're doing all this hard work!

Business plans keep you on the right track, and they replenish your core enthusiasm and vision for your business if you ever feel (and sometimes you will!) that it's all getting a bit too much.

Law 31: A business plan is your calling card.
It gives you external credibility

One of the main reasons why people need a business plan is for use as a sales vehicle to raise money. But don't confuse the business with the business plan. In the words of Arthur Rock, the great enture capitalist who sees 300 business plans a year: "Good ideas and good products are dime a dozen. Good execution and good management – in a word, good people – are rare. To put it another way strategy is easy, but tactics – the day-to-day and month-to month decisions required to manage a business – are hard. That is why I generally pay more attention to the people behind the business plan than to the proposal itself."

Dot.com market legend has it that millions were raised on the basis of calculations hastily written on a British Rail napkin! A business plan would have been better as, perhaps, many investors are now finding out to their cost.

WHO SHOULD WRITE THE BUSINESS PLAN?

Remember our rule for market research in the last chapter. You have to do it. The same rule rears its head again here. Writing a business plan is YOUR job. And the reasons for that are largely the same as they were last time, too.

You know the product and market better than anyone else. You are the one with the enthusiasm and the commitment, and this will shine through in the document you write. Someone who is not intimate with the idea will not produce a compelling business plan. The document needs to convey the enthusiasm and energy of the entrepreneurs and this is unlikely if it is written on your behalf by a professional adviser.

Also, like market research, inspiration comes while you are working. The process of writing will help you to focus on your vision and start the step-by-step process of how you will turn that vision into reality.

And you don't need any special skills. Everything you need to write the business plan is in your head already. Sahar was, at first, very intimidated about the idea of writing the Coffee Republic business plan and worried that with no business training or knowledge she was not capable of producing an effective one. She told Bobby to give her a year to go to business school before she could undertake such a task. But she began anyway and soon realised how fulfilling it was to nail down all the abstract thoughts
that had been randomly tossed about and to put them into a concrete document. The brain dump proved quite therapeutic!

She discovered that even for the financial projections (a very alien and frightening area for her) you don't necessarily need investment banking training to figure it all out. She had already gathered the numbers in the research stage so all she needed was a pad of paper, a calculator, a lot of guesswork and a measure of hard work.

However Sahar couldn't have done it without Bobby's guidance through the numbers stage. So if you shrivel at the mention of figures, consider getting a professional to analyse them for you and help you to produce a more professional plan (The Prince's Trust, Business Link and other government organisations give free advice). Another great idea is to bring on board a financial partner for your venture, a Bobby. In that way you can have someone who is committed to your business doing the figures, but one whom you don't need to pay.

WHAT SHOULD BE IN YOUR BUSINESS PLAN?

There are so many books and guides on writing business plans that we won't mention specific details here. But there is a simple Anyone Can Do It way of approaching the outline of a business plan.

BASICALLY A BUSINESS PLAN IS A FAIRLY DETAILED EXPLANATION OF:

- What you plan to do
  (that great idea that you are passionate about).

- Why you think it will work given the market, competition and customer demand *(remember all that market research you did? Express your conviction to convince others here).*

- Why you are the right person to execute the business plan and bring the concept into reality *(your CV and how you propose to deal with any gaps in your experience).*

- How will your business make money? *(Are your price and volumes high enough to cover all your costs?)*

- How much money you need to get started *(your set up costs and the working capital needed to keep your business running).*

We will end this chapter with a copy of our original business plan. We started writing it on 29 November 1994, less than a month after we first discussed the idea. Yes, bits of it are very out of date but looking back, it was a sincere and honest document that accurately outlined our original vision for Coffee Republic.

But our last word on the business plan stage is this: don't get too bogged down in the search for perfection. A successful business on paper doesn't necessarily translate into a successful business in the real world. Great business plans don't necessarily make great businesses. Do the best business plan you can, but save your real energy for rolling up your sleeves up and actually doing it.

JAVA EXPRESS

COFFEE & ESPRESSO BAR

BUSINESS PLAN

February 1995

I. EXECUTIVE SUMMARY

Java Express is a specialty espresso bar concept based on a broad and creative
selection of espresso based coffee beverages. Java Express provides a new coffee
experience by creating a "context" for enjoying specialty coffee beverages and making
coffee drinking an end in itself. This concept is different to anything present in the
U.K. coffee bar market today.

Java Express offers its customers not just cappuccino or espresso, but a host of
exciting high quality espresso concoctions with names like caffe latte, caffe mocha and
macchiato. These drinks are created and served by trained "Baristas" who act more
like skilled cocktail barmen than your average coffee bar employee. The Baristas will
offer these drinks by mixing espresso with steamed or foamed milk, chocolate,
flavorings, or whipped cream in varying amounts depending on the type of drink
ordered and the customer's specific request. As a compliment to the coffee offerings,
Java Express will also serve an assortment of teas, juices, cakes, muffins and bagels.

The Java Express concept first started in Seattle, and is currently spreading rapidly
throughout the U.S. by hundreds of expanding specialty coffee bar chains, the best
known of which is Starbucks, also referred to as the "Liquid McDonalds". Starbucks
has expanded from 17 espresso bars in 1987 to more than 425 bars today, and
continues to expand at the rate of two new bar openings a week. And yet there is still
scope for smaller entrants in the market. For example, a New York based coffee chain
founded by a close friend of the management opened its first store in March 1993 and
now in the space of two years owns 14 stores, and is still expanding rapidly.

As yet, no one has brought this concept to the U.K. It seems that the leading U.S.
companies in this business are far too busy expanding in the U.S. to concentrate on the
market here. There is thus an opportunity to lead the trend in the enormous U.K.
market - this is the opportunity Java Express intends to exploit.

The U.K. specialty coffee beverage market is still dominated by the traditional Italian
sandwich bars who serve mediocre coffee - the atmosphere is focused on food and not
coffee. And yet the average London Italian sandwich bar sells about 500-600
cappuccinos a day; for example, Ponti's in Covent Garden, which is a food bar rather
than a coffee bar, manages to sell 6,000 cappuccinos on a Saturday.

But times are changing and the domination of these Italian sandwich bars is rapidly
being eroded by new food retailing concepts such as Pret a Manger. But no one has
yet challenged the sandwich bars on the coffee.

There has been some recent press coverage about the new "coffee craze" in the U.K.
Costa Coffee, the only major coffee bar chain, manages to sell 700 cappuccinos in the
lunch period every day in Moorgate. Successful cart operations have also started in
the Broadgate centre and manage to sell a thousand cappuccinos a day. More
generally, the gap between tea and coffee drinking has been steadily reducing in the

U.K. - ground coffee is considered one of the most buoyant sectors in the U.K. beverage market.

In view of the tremendous potential in the U.K. market and the huge success of this concept in the U.S., Java Express is committed to establishing itself not as just another coffee shop, but as a leading <u>brand</u> of espresso bar concept in the U.K.

Management would like to emphasizes that any current food bar or coffee bar on the market today can instantly decide to offer a wider choice of flavored espresso beverages. But what differentiates Java Express from its competitors (including Aroma for example, which already has an extensive coffee menu) is that Java Express provides a unique "package" - the crucial combination of all the elements of the Company's strategy that result in a truly unique customer experience and engenders customer loyalty.

The following 5 primary elements are the unique selling points that differentiate Java Express from its competitors, and fosters customer loyalty. These elements will cushion Java Express against a proliferation of espresso bars similiar to the U.S phenomenon:

1. High quality product offerings
2. Superior customer service
3. Unique merchandising and marketing
4. Convenient store locations
5. Distinctive shop design and atmosphere

The management of the Company has been structured to provide investors with confidence and a range of skills and experience necessary to meet the needs of this business.

Although the short term focus of the management is to implement this concept in a first retail outfit of less than 300 square feet, the long term goal is to pursue an aggressive expansion strategy in both existing and new markets in order to realize operating and marketing economies of scale and create a powerful brand identity.

II. BUSINESS

A. COMPANY OVERVIEW & STRATEGY

Java Express is a specialty coffee bar concept offering a broad and creative selection of Italian style coffee beverages at convenient and accessible locations in the City. Java Express provides its customers with a new coffee experience by creating a "context" for enjoying specialty coffee beverages and making coffee drinking an end in itself.

Java Express is different to anything present in the U.K. coffee bar market today- it is based on the specialty espresso bar concept which started in Seattle, and is currently spreading rapidly throughout the U.S. These bars are very different from the traditional food/coffee bars, and focus solely on coffee, offering an extensive menu of high quality espresso concoctions with names like caffe latte, caffe mocha and macchiato.

The Company's short term goal is to implement this concept in a first retail outfit of less than 300 square feet. The Company's medium term goal is to pursue an aggressive expansion strategy in both London and other major U.K. cities in order to create a powerful brand identity. The Company's long term goal is to become the leading brand of specialty espresso bars in the U.K.

Management would like to emphasizes that any current food bar or coffee bar on the market today can instantly decide to offer a wider choice of flavored espresso beverages. But what differentiates Java Express from its competitors (including Aroma for example, which already has an extensive coffee menu) is that Java Express provides a unique "package" - the crucial combination of all the elements of the Company's strategy that result in a truly unique customer experience and engenders customer loyalty.

The following 5 primary elements are the unique selling points that differentiate Java Express from its competitors, and fosters customer loyalty. These elements will cushion Java Express against a proliferation of espresso bars similiar to the U.S phenomenon.

High Quality Product Offerings. Java Express is dedicated to providing coffee of the highest quality. The Company's product offerings will meet the needs of its customers for premium quality coffee beverages in a fast paced business environment. The recipes for its coffee blends and food offerings are all developed with the objective of having distinctive and superior products as compared to its competitors. Although Java Express' image and sales are led by coffee, it will also offer other products which serve as a complement to coffee in order to entice customers to visit many times per day.

Customer Service. The Company's goal is to develop a positive and pro-active customer service approach which results in customers who are pleased every time they visit a Java Express bar. Since the specialty coffee bar concept is new in the U.K., and the Company relies on a high rate of repeat business, it views the quality of its customer interaction with its employees as critical to its success, with employees playing a crucial role in informing the customers about the array of choices available. Through its emphasis on training, personnel development and profit-sharing compensation, the Company intends to attract well qualified, highly motivated employees committed to providing superior levels of customer service.

Merchandising and Marketing. The Company will implement an aggressive merchandising and marketing strategy designed to create and reinforce a distinctive brand image built on the quality of its product offerings. The Company will extensively use the Java Express logo on its innovative product presentation, packaging and leaflets. In addition, employees will offer customers a variety of creative marketing concepts such as free samples of "flavor-of-the-day" espresso shots, frequent-drinker cards, and a host of coffee educational material, including colourful promotional posters and T-shirts.

Store Location. Since the convenience of a coffee bar is a critical element in attracting customers, the location of shops has been a primary criteria in site selection. Our site selection strategy is to open outlets in high-traffic, high-visibility locations in commercial areas, preferably not far from other food serving establishments such as Marks & Spencers or Boots.

Shop design and atmosphere. Java Express will be designed along the lines of the U.S espresso bars, with floor-to-ceiling windows, suggesting a sense of simple and clean sophistication, style, comfort, warmth and environmental awareness. The bars will be able to accommodate a high volume of traffic while retaining an inviting and casual atmosphere. The bars will have stand up counters against the walls, and limited bar seating. The distinctive shop design and decor will visually reinforce the difference between Java Express and its competitors and further reinforce Java Express' brand image.

B. PRODUCT OFFERINGS

While the Company's menu is primarily focused on coffee, it will also offer other selected beverages and coffee cakes and snacks which serve as a complement to coffee.

1. Coffee Beverages

Java Express offers Italian style espresso beverages, both caffeinated and decaffeinated, which include *espresso, caffe latte, cappucino, caffe mocha, and espresso macchiato*. These espresso drinks combine espresso with foamed or steamed milk, chocolate, flavourings or whipped cream in varying amounts depending on the type of drink ordered and also the customer's specific request. The Company caters to individual preferences by offering a choice of regular, semi-skimmed and skimmed milk. All the espresso beverages are also available on ice in order to maintain consistent sales during the warm weather.

Customers will be able to help themselves to vanilla, cocoa, cinnamon and nutmeg cappuccino shakers as well as different sugars and also honey as a healthy sugar alternative.

2. Other Beverages

Java Express will offer the following beverages:
1. Teas: A variety of teas including classic, exotic flavours and fruit teas.
2. Fresh Fruit Juices: Orange and Grapefruit.
3. Mineral Water: Still and gaseous.

3. Coffee Cakes & Snacks

Java Express will offer a broad selection of high quality pastries. These include loaf cakes, muffins, croissants and bagels with cream cheese. In order to create a niche in the health conscious fast food market, fat-free low calorie muffins and cakes will also be offered.

C. PRICING

Java Express prices its coffee and other products competitively with the prevailing high-end coffee prices reflecting the high quality of the coffee and its high level of customer service.

The following basic retail price categories are suggested. Customers will be charged extra for specials, custom made beverages and additional shots of espresso, whipped cream or flavorings:

•	Cappucino	1.20 pounds
•	Espresso	1.00
•	Tea	0.60
•	Juices	1.00
•	Cake Serving	1.00

REVISED

Although relative prices are higher in the US espresso bars, such as $1.89 for a cappuccino, the Company does not believe that it can charge more for a regular cappuccino for two reasons: a) the US market is different to the extent people do not mind paying a premium for having the prestige factor of buying their coffee from a specialty store, and b) the Company is targeting U.K. office workers who are typically budget conscious.

The Company will train it's Baristas to implement "up-selling" - where customers are actively encouraged to try new combinations and add extras to a single drink, such as extra shots of espresso, flavouring or topping of whipped cream. Although the price of the basic drink is competitive, these extras will increase high-margin sales.

D. MERCHANDISING & MARKETING

The Company's marketing strategy is to create brand awareness, encourage trial purchases by educating customers about the selections available, and promote repeat business by reinforcing positive experiences through the Company's product mix and friendly service.

Implementation of this strategy will include the following elements:

- Offering free samples to allow customers to try "taste-of-the-day" concoctions they would not otherwise choose.
- 2-for-1 cards which can only be used on separate days - encouraging multiple visits.
- Frequent-Drinker Cards. These will have 10 stamp marks which will be stamped every time the card holder buys a coffee. When the card is filled, the holder gets a free drink.
- Educational material (posters or leaflets) about quality of coffee, its benefits and guide to various espresso drinks, and the Company's mission statement - including a money-back guarantee.
- Employee pro-active service & marketing: Educating and training employees about preparation of beverages and enthusiastic customer service. Java Express employees will be genuinely "excited" about the unique selling concepts and actively promote and relay this enthusiasm to customers.
- Free delivery to nearby offices
- Java Express stores will have logos on the windows, awnings and walls, acting as advertising billboards at the shop's high-visibility location.

Another crucial element in Java Express' merchandising strategy is its unique product presentation through high quality take-away cups. These cups will be superior to the lower quality polystyrene cups provided by sandwich bars. They will be sturdy, practical, and decorated with the Company logo. The cups will be identical to those supplied by the US coffee shops and will be supplied by the same company. The lids will also be unique, enabling the drinker to drink without taking off the lid or spilling their drink. The company believes its cups are essential in creating the company's brand image and reinforcing its difference with its competitors.

Management expects word-of mouth and foot traffic to be sufficient to allow our stores to become profitable.

E. CUSTOMER SERVICE

Java Express will carry out internal marketing to successfully hire, train, and motivate able employees to serve customers enthusiastically and to make them fully understand the impact they have on customer satisfaction. The 'Americanized' customer service and attitude of employees will be another important factor in distinguishing Java Express from its competitors and establishing the brand image.

All employees will be trained with emphasis on knowledge of coffee and beverage preparation and should act as messengers of the Seattle coffee bar concept to educate clients as to the new culture by helping clients choose and enthusiastically recommending new drinks- especially as such a huge choice of espresso beverages and catering to customer's individual needs (e.g. type of milk) is new in the U.K.

All employees will be outfitted with trendy, upbeat but clean and healthy looking uniforms. This will consist initially of attractive T-shirts carrying the company colour and logo, and jeans.

F. STORE DESIGN

Java Express will be designed along the lines of the U.S espresso bars, with floor-to-ceiling windows, suggesting a sense of simple and clean sophistication, style, comfort, warmth and environmental awareness. The bars will be able to accommodate a high volume of traffic while retaining an inviting and casual atmosphere. The bars will have stand up counters against the walls, and limited bar seating. The distinctive shop design and decor will visually reinforce the difference between Java Express and its competitors and further reinforce Java Express' brand image.

The Company has already engaged Househam Henderson Architects to provide a budget cost for shop design and shop fitting expenses.

G. SITE SELECTION AND LOCATION

Java Express' site selection strategy is to open stores in high-traffic, high-visibility locations as customers will rarely walk more than 2 blocks out of their way to buy coffee. The ideal location is business districts or densely populated retail areas. In order to capture and serve a bigger share of the market, Java Express will establish a number of proximate stores rather than a single large store that customers would have to go out of their way to patronize.

Java Express has specific site selection criteria. The Company prefers to locate near a busy tube station or within the path from the tube station. Alternatively, the location has to be near big commercial retailers e.g. Marks & Spencers or Boots.

In evaluating a potential location the company studies an area within two blocks as it believes it will draw a majority of its customers from a 2 block radius. This area represents the market area in which the Company believes each Java Express competes.

Information is obtained on all competitors within that area. The Company evaluates the Company's ability to establish a dominant presence in that area, in order to create entry barriers to other competitors. The Company believes that it can secure an area where it can have a captive market and enjoy repeat cycle of business. The Company collects pedestrian count information and sales are projected based on this information.

H. SUPPLIES

Coffee

Other Offerings

I. SHOP OPERATIONS AND MANAGEMENT

The shop will be staffed by one shop manager who will work full-time and two hourly workers working on a part-time basis. The Company anticipates that at any given time it is necessary to only have 2 employees - one to take orders and collect money, and the other at the coffee machine.

All employees will have to wear Java Express uniforms.

The opening hours are 7:00 am to 6:00 pm; 5 business days per week..

III. MARKET

In terms of studying the market for the Java Express concept, we have considered the following two markets to be relevant:

1) The Fast Food market
2) The UK Coffee Market

1) THE FAST FOOD MARKET

The activities of Java Express fall into the fast food market. The general trends and recent developments within this market indicate favourable conditions for the establishment of the Java Express concept. In summary these are:

i)   The size of the market and its potential for growth
ii)   The new trends and recent developments in the sector
iii) The tremendous opportunities for innovative small players
iv)   The coffee craze
v)   The change in people's eating habits

i) The size of the market and its potential for growth

The U.K. fast food trade constitutes a significant sector in the U.K. consumer catering market, accounting for a 34% share with retail sales of 4.7 billion pounds in 1993. Over the period 1988 to 1993, the market grew by 32%. The overall prospects for the U.K. fast food sector look particularly bright, and the market is likely to benefit from the growing trends towards convenience food and the overall increased affluence, which will foster the eating out habit . This sector is forecasted to grow at a 4% rate from 4.7 billion pounds in 1993 to 5.7 billion pounds in 1998.

Within the fast food market, Java Express seeks to serve the sandwich sector. It is from sandwich shops that most people buy their take away coffees in London. The sandwich sector is the largest sector of the fast food market, with estimated sales in 1993 of 1.5 billion pounds, and a market share of 32%, well ahead of hamburgers with 18% and pizzas with 14%. According to the British Sandwich Association, consumers buy more than 40 million sandwiches a week. The London market alone accounts for approximately 350 million pounds. On a daily basis sandwich bars have more customers than McDonald's, Burger King, Pizza Hut and Pizza Land put together.

ii) The trends and recent developments in the sandwich sector

The sandwich sector has long been dominated by traditional Italian sandwich bars which also serve beverages including coffee. There are more than 3,000 independent sandwich bars in London. However in the last five years there has been a new trend in the market. The dominance of these Italian bars on the sandwich side is coming under increasing pressure from the likes of Boots and Marks & Spencer who have opened extremely successful sandwich operations. The Marks & Spencers sandwich shop in Moorgate sells an estimated 3.5 million sandwiches per year.

This market trend is very favourable to Java Express. Since these grocery multiples do not serve coffee or any other hot beverages, there now exists an enormous body of customers who have to go elsewhere to buy coffee. These customers would obviously prefer a specialty coffee bar and avoid queues at places that are also serving food. This is a niche Java Express aims to exploit.

iii) The opportunities for innovative small players

Recently the market has witnessed the immense success of a new entrant, Pret a Manger, to the sector. Pret a Manger has opened 27 branches in the last four years and has doubled its turnover in two years to 10 million pounds. To open their first shop in Holborn in 1990, Pret a Manger got a 100,000 pound bank loan. It was projected that they break even in 6 months and repay in five years. They broke even on the third day of trading and repaid the loan in 15 months. Since then they have been to the bank 14 times and always exceed their projections.

The enormous success of Pret a Manger has two advantages for Java Express. Firstly, it has provided a further and more damaging threat to the traditional sandwich bar. Secondly, their rapid expansion indicates how buoyant the market is and indicates that scope still exists for the innovative small player.

Another important factor to consider is that despite the new trends, the traditional sandwich bars have taken a declining share of the market, yet their actual level of sales have not declined. This stresses the enormous potential within this buoyant market.

iv) The Coffee Craze

A recent article in the Independent newspaper refers to the recent "coffee craze" in the UK and the booming cafe society and how the "British have rediscovered the joys of arabica beans". A recent Financial Times article about Espresso a la Carte refers to the franchise potential of espresso carts. A Time Out article explains the creation of Seattle style concoctions. This recent press interest is paralleled with the success of the following specialty coffee bars:

The largest chain of outlets selling only coffee are the Costa Coffee Boutiques run by the established coffee suppliers, Costa Brothers. Costa has 14 branches in London mostly in tube and British Rail stations and have major presence in the airports. Costa Coffee in Liverpool Street sells an average of 700-800 cups during lunch alone each day.

Aroma, another new food/sandwich chain with more emphasis on coffee has also had success in the last few years with 5 branches. It has opened a branch in Books Etc retail bookstore in Charing Cross following the current US trend of placing coffee shops in book stores.

Espresso a la Carte has introduced the Seattle espresso carts concept to London. It has 3 carts in Broadgate Centre and also Victoria Station - its 3 carts in Broadgate sell about 1,000 espresso beverages a day. A recent Financial Times article estimates its annual turnover from four carts at approximately 1.5 million pounds.

v) The changing eating habits

Market reports indicate that the general trend has been an increase in snacking and eating between meals. With the erosion of family mealtimes there has been greater demand for convenience foods.

There is also reference in the reports to the health conscious fast food eater.

2. THE U.K. COFFEE MARKET

Most figures relate to retail sector coffee sales rather than coffee beverages sales. Although this is not directly relevant to Java Express' activities, management feels that it is the most accurate barometer of consumer tastes.

Coffee is the world's largest exported commodity after oil. The U.K. has the EC's lowest per capita consumption of coffee. However the U.K. consumption is steadily increasing , the scope for further growth being illustrated by a comparison of coffee consumption in other countries.

- U.K.   2.6 kg of coffee per capita per year
- USA   4.3 kg of coffee per capita per year
- France   5.7 kg of coffee per capita per year
- Finland   13.3 kg of coffee per capita per year

(Figures derived from International Coffee Organization Report)

Coffee consumption is divided into two sectors: a) instant and b) real (ie. whole beans or ground coffee). Instant coffee accounts for 91% of total U.K. coffee consumption. U.K. has EC's lowest consumption of real coffee with 0.4 kg of real coffee consumed per person. This compares to France, where 90% of the population drinks real coffee with 4.4 kg of real coffee per person. In Finland consumption is 10 kg of real coffee per head.

But although these figures are low, there has been a significantly upward trend in the U.K. consumption of coffee with volume sales increasing steadily by 3% annually. Although tea still remains the national beverage, the gap between tea and coffee is steadily reducing.

The increase in the U.K. consumption has been mainly in the real coffee market, whereas instant coffee sales have remained static. The real coffee sector is one of the most buoyant in the beverage market. The high activity in this market has attracted European companies, further indicating the extent of the U.K. real coffee market's growth potential.

The trend in the market is that with the increase in foreign travel, the British are becoming more conscious of the quality of their coffee. This is also reflected by the increase of raw imports of top quality arabica beans and a decrease in the lower quality robusta beans.

London accounts for 25% total U.K. real coffee consumption, and for 40% total U.K. espresso consumption. 63% of real coffee is drunk away from home mostly at work.

Further evidence of the upward trend in real coffee consumption can be evidenced by the recent success of Whittards, retailer of fine tea and coffee. In four years it has expanded from 3 to 32 shops with a 7 million pound turnover.

IV. CUSTOMERS

Java Express' target customers are office workers, both professional and non-professional, covering a wide range of ages and income levels, who are time-sensitive, yet appreciate a higher quality coffee experience than is typically found at typical food/sandwich bars. The stores will be located to be accessible for office workers on their way to work in the morning and/or during their lunch hour either to buy lunch or run errands.

The company expects to enjoy a high degree of repeat business, i.e. that a majority of its customers will come in more than once a week.

The Company expects 75% of its customers to order for take away. This figure is confirmed at Pret a Manger as an example, where only 25% of its customers choose to eat at the bars.

The Company also wants to target the health-conscious and the weight-conscious customer by offering skimmed milk and fat free and healthy muffins.

The Company also aims to create a niche with environmentally conscious customers through its store design and packaging.

V. COMPETITION

The Company believes that the principal competitive factors in the specialty coffee bar market are quality of products, service, brand name recognition, and store location.

Java Express will compete directly against all food/sandwich bars, and beverage outlets that serve coffee. In evaluating the market area in which each store will compete, the Company will study the area within two blocks radius.

At present, Java Express' competitors in the London fast food breakfast/lunch market are :

1. Traditional Food/Sandwich Bars

Office Canteen/Restaurants:

2. New Concept Food/Sandwich Bars

Pret a Manger:

Croissant Express and Croissant Shops:

3. Specialty Coffee Bars

Costa Coffee boutiques:

Aroma:

Espresso a la Carte:

4. Potential Competition

With the growing trend of specialty coffee bars in the U.S., the untapped market in the U.K. is likely to attract interest from those coffee bars already established in the U.S. and other individuals who realize the same opportunity. At the moment, U.S. coffee bar chains are too busy with U.S. expansion in order to consider expansion to the U.K.

Java Express plans to establish itself as a recognized brand of espresso bar before any major U.S. companies expand into the U.K. market.

VI. MANAGEMENT

The management structure provides the following range of skills and experience:

a) Professionalism (see backgrounds below).
b) The espresso bar concept is an American concept that has to be adapted to the sensitive British market. The cultural composition of management (one British and one American) is unique to deal with this adaptation and to bridge the gap of the two cultures.
c) Finance, management, entrepreneurial and legal skills.
d) Extensive contacts in USA espresso bar market.
e) A balance of personal attributes including initiative, ambition and determination and unquestioned integrity.

Sahar Hashemi Age 27, is a solicitor by profession with 5 years experience in corporate and commercial law at a reputable City firm. Having worked in prime city locations over many years, she is fully aware with first hand experience of the needs of the market.

Miss Hashemi is responsible for the Company's marketing, operations, legal matters, and site and lease procurement.

Babak Hashemi Age 31, is an investment banker by profession, having worked at Lehman Brothers in New York. Mr. Hashemi obtained an MBA degree from Dartmouth College in the U.S and has strong management and entrepreneurial skills together with the finance skills he acquired in investment banking.. Prior to his MBA, he trained as an engineer at IBM and General Electric, followed by a career in finance and strategic planning at Ultramar PLC in New York.

Mr. Hashemi is responsible for the Company's overall financial management, including financing, budgeting, accounting, and cash management.

The management is closely connected with the CEO and founder of a highly successful and expanding chain of espresso bars on the East coast with 20 branches opened in 2 years. The CEO of this espresso bar chain has provided us unlimited help from his experiences in setting up such a successful operation, and we believe our unique relationship will be an invaluable asset for us.

Since embarking on this new venture, Messrs. Hashemi have visited New York twice as part of their research, spending considerable time at various New York espresso bar stores.

Neither Miss Sahar Hashemi or Mr. Babak Hashemi have any prior experience in the food retail sector. As such, the store will be managed by a full time store manger with sufficient coffee bar experience.

The hourly employees will be selected on the basis of coffee machine experience and enthusiasm about the Java Express concept. The Company will hire between one to two hourly employees depending on the size and traffic volumes.

All employees will undergo a two-day coffee training course.

Management intends to attract and motivate the highest quality employees by offering profit sharing incentives to our store managers, effectively making them partners in the company's profits and success.

VII. FINANCIAL PROJECTIONS

Capital Costs
Management expects to lease and fit a prime retail space of approximately 250 square feet. Summarized capital costs are forecasted as follows.

• Lease Costs	29,500	(includes 25,000 pound lease deposit)
• Shop Fittings	24,875	
• Coffee Machines	4,982	
• Equipment	2,376	
• Misc.	1,100	
• Total	62,833	

In addition, management will need to secure a 15,000 pound working capital facility for first year operating cash flow balances. This facility is steadily reduced throughout the first year, and will no longer be required during the second year.

Sales
The assumptions are based on the performance of 1 Espresso Bar throughout the year. Management conservatively assumes first month sales based on 200 visitors per day, escalating gradually over a period of 6 months to a steady state of 500 visitors per day, resulting in an average annual rate of 413 visitors per day, and 523 pounds per square foot. During the second year, average monthly sales are forecasted to exceed 600 visitors per day.

Based on management's research, the average London Italian sandwich bar sells about 500-600 cappuccinos a day. Ponti's in Covent Garden, which is a restaurant rather than a coffee bar sells 6,000 cappuccinos on a Saturday alone. Costa Coffee, the only coffee bar chain, manages to sell 700 cappuccinos in the lunch period every day in Moorgate. Cart operations in the Broadgate centre manage to sell 1,000 cappuccinos per day.

Product Mix
Management assumes that 75% of visitors will order Cappuccino-based drinks, and approximately 25% will order Espresso or Tea. In addition, approximately 30% of visitors will also order pastries or a cold drink such as orange juice.

Salaries
Management will hire an experienced full-time store manager at 15,000 pounds per year, and two hourly rotating assistants at 4.00 pounds/hour.

Financial Performance

The Espresso Bar has forecasted sales of 130,655 pounds, operating cash flow of 15,909 pounds, and net cash flow (net of interest and taxes) of 7,483 pounds. Operating cash flow generated is approximately twice the monthly interest expense.

Gross margin	73%
Operating Cash Flow / Sales	12%
Operating Cash Flow / Interest	200%
Operating Cash Flow / Investment	25%

CHAPTER FIVE:
RAISING MONEY FOR YOUR IDEA
TURNING THE IDEA INTO A BUSINESS

Law 32: Raising money is the first critical sale
you have to make

Until now, your time has been spent in convincing yourself about the viability of your business. You've researched your idea and formalised it in a business plan. Now is the time that you use your newly acquired conviction to actually persuade other business people that your prospects are good so that they will give you the financial support you require. You've reached the point when, for the first time, you have to sell your idea.

It won't be easy. Remember the dot.com business plans on British Rail napkins? We can pretty much guarantee that you're going to need a lot more than that if you want to raise funds successfully. You will need to be organised, persuasive and very persistent. Our 'raising money' phase was a time when we really had to draw on our bank of commitment. As you set about raising finance, here are the questions that you will need to answer.

How much money will you need?
Once you've done the business plan and financial projections as we did, you'll find that you will have a good idea of how much money will be required to launch your business.

We needed money for:

i) Setting up costs for our first coffee bar: the 'once in a lifetime expense' of leasing, design and build, and opening of our first store. We estimated that on a 250 sq. ft. property, our costs would be £64,000 which included:

Lease costs: £30,000 (including a £25,000 lease deposit).
Shop fitting: £25,000.
Coffee machines and Equipment: £7,400.
Miscellaneous: £1,100

ii) Working capital.
This was the money we would need to keep the business going in the unavoidable time gap between paying out cash for supplies, employees' wages and loan repayments, and actually getting in cash from customers.

Since all our customers paid cash, we had a 'cash business' which would mean we would have money coming in from day one, and since we didn't need to hold a big stock of goods either, our working capital requirements were relatively small. We calculated that we would need £15,000 working capital to cover our first full year of operations.

So, in total we needed £90,000 to open the first branch of Coffee Republic.

These figures were all educated guesses based on a 'typical' scenario. We hadn't even found a site when we put them together. So we based different versions of the proposal on different sites and had to change things each time we failed to get a site that we had targeted.

Law 33: Strike a fine balance being conservative and ambitious

Law 34: Write a plan you can beat

The balance that we had to maintain was between being too conservative in our assumptions so we wouldn't have to go back for more money within a short time, and making the business proposition exciting and viable enough to attract the money we needed. As a result, we steered the middle course. Our actual goal was 'beat our plan'. In other words, we were aiming for higher sales and lower costs than we projected on paper.

Where do you raise the money?
It is a bizarre fact about raising money that it's actually easier to come up with very large sums of over £1m than the smaller sums that most start-ups need.

Bobby had had plenty of experience raising millions for his clients in investment banking but when Sahar approached him with the question which she thought would be a piece of cake for him, she was surprised to find that he had no idea how to raise £90,000.

Law 35: 90% of start-ups are financed by the guts, creativity and faith of the founders

You should look at money issues not as dry, boring, business problems but as marketing challenges. So we set about being entrepreneurial in our approach to raising money. First we did some research. We read the relevant chapters in the 'how to start a business' guides (like the LloydsTSB Small Business Guide) to find a way to raise our £90,000. The first thing these guides advised us to decide was what type of finance was appropriate: lending (a straightforward bank loan where you pay interest in return for borrowing money), or equity (giving away a portion of your business in return for an investment).

Each type of finance has its advantages and disadvantages. Bobby knew from experience that for a start-up, giving away equity has many more disadvantages than a straightforward loan. As yet your business doesn't have much value so you don't have much leverage in negotiations and end up giving away more of the business than you would like to raise the money you need.

As a result, we decided that getting a 'plain vanilla' loan from a high street bank was the best option for us.

The problem with this approach is that a 'plain vanilla' loan means that the bank needs security against the amount they're giving you and since we had no assets to offer as security, our only option was a personal guarantee. We desperately wanted to avoid giving a personal guarantee because we both strongly believed what Sahar had been taught as a lawyer: that 'the definition of a personal guarantor is a fool with a pen'.

To try to avoid this, we approached the lack of security dilemma creatively and searched for a solution. In the end, in a 'How to Start a Business' textbook, we learned about the Small Firms Loan Guarantee Scheme which helps new businesses that cannot get a conventional loan because of a lack of security.

Under the scheme, the DTI provides security by guaranteeing seventy percent of the loan. We investigated the details and found to our enormous relief that we qualified. So with our security problem resolved, we approached the banks.

As we said, we tried the high street banks. Because we had no close personal links with any particular one (a broad collection of overdrafts notwithstanding), we approached all of them. We were amazed to discover that each separate branch of a bank operates under its own rules, so because one branch of a high street bank rejects you, it does not mean that you'll get the same answer at another. Each manager has his or her own discretionary lending limit so you can shop around until you've had as much rejection as you can bear.

We wrote to all the major high street banks randomly: Lloyds, Midland, NatWest, Barclays, Clydesdale, the Royal Bank of Scotland. We simply called 192 (directory enquiries) and randomly asked for different branches of different banks that came into our heads: "Midland Bank on High Street Ken...Barclays on Fleet Street...Lloyds Bank on the Strand..."

Law 36: Be prepared for rejection and disapointment

And as we were rejected by each branch that we arbitrarily contacted, we simply tried another.

FINANCIALS: FIN BUSINESS PLAN: BP EXECUTIVE SUMMARY: ES INSTITUTIONS	SUBMITTED VERSION 1	VERSION 1.5	VERSION 2	VERSION 3	VERSION 4
COUTTS	(RETURNED UNFEES) BP/FIN 9/FEB	~~SECOND REJECT~~			
NATWEST	ES/FIN 14/FEB BP(+10 FIN) 20/FEB		FIN 27/FEB	11/MARCH	14/MARCH
BARCLAY	BP/FIN 10/FEB		2/3/95.	REJECTED	
MIDLAND	BP/FIN 9/FEB	FIN BP 16/FEB	10/3/95		
CLYDSDALE	ES/FIN 11/FEB NO INTEREST 10/FEB				
ROYAL BANK OF SCOTLAND	~~BP/FIN~~ —	BP/FIN 16/FEB	REJECTED		
LLOYDS	BP/FIN 7/FEB		2/3/95		

And what did we get for our troubles? In total, a glorious pile of paper made up of twenty-two separate rejections. It was a very demoralising task, as one bank manager after another told us that our idea would not work!

Some rejected us on the basis of our cover letter and the business plan we had sent, others met us and then rejected us after hearing our presentation. It was more heart wrenching being rejected after face-to-face encounters as we had put so much energy and enthusiasm into our presentations.

We hope these replies serve as comfort for any would-be entrepreneurs against the barrage of lack of interest and belief you will get:

- "The English will never order fancy coffee names."

- "I found a 45p cappuccino on Fleet Street."

- "You two are too inexperienced in the catering world to make it work."

- "Good idea, but sorry. It's not for us."

- "There are too many sandwich bars already."

- "You two have no idea what's out there already."

- "We're a nation of tea drinkers – coffee is a fad."

- "We can't understand how you're different from any other coffee bar."

Just had a call from ▇▇▇▇▇▇▇▇▇▇▇ He said he has to refuse on the grounds
1. Borrowing is too much
2. He has been to Fleet Street site and doesn't like it. Too close to Di Lietos and should be further up the street
3. Price of Capp. too high as he went around Fleet street and found 45p cappuccinos 🔲 ← Dickhea

Basically as I told you when we met him I am not surprised. He is such a pea minded ▇▇▇▇▇▇▇ He was off to france this afternoon and I got the impression he just wanted to clear his desk ie. not have to worry about anything else during one of his many holidays.

I will ring a west end ▇▇▇▇ to try again.

Midland , I am typing a draft response and will send it ti yoiu.

mr
▇▇▇▇
with
pins
stuck
in him.

We're almost tempted to say that if your idea generates a good few refusals, then you have another reason to believe that you're on to something good!

Never forget that you are a pioneer in uncharted waters and if what you are doing were so easy then everyone else would be doing it too. Its the hard that makes it so great.

With no fewer than three rejections from NatWest alone, we wrote to a Mr. Lindop, the manager of the Chancery Lane branch for the questionably good reason that Sahar suddenly decided that as she'd been to Law School in Chancery Lane, perhaps this would be our lucky bank. Believe it or not it was! Or perhaps we'd worked hard enough to deserve the lucky break finally coming our way.

For some unknown reason, Mr Lindop wanted to give us a chance. They say never judge by appearances, and he was proof of this. The Chancery Lane branch of NatWest is straight out of a Dickens novel; small, dark and dustily antique in feeling. Mr Lindop was a shy retiring man of the classic, ashen constitution; the last person you would ever imagine backing a new venture that absolutely everyone else had rejected. When, in your head, you imagine a 'bank manager' Mr. Lindop, believe us, is the person you see!

We gave him a full presentation, even showing him Sahar's New York album to give him a real flavour for the concept. He was so detached and glacial that we had no idea what he thought but there was earnestness about him that we liked.

The telltale sign might have been that (with hindsight) he was the first one who didn't tell us how it couldn't be done. Mr Lindop just listened to us with interest.

It was finally on 27 March that he wrote to us agreeing in principle to the loan.

The dilemma now was that the loan was conditional on him approving the site and we still hadn't found one! We still therefore had a significant hurdle to overcome. It was a classic chicken-and-egg dilemma that reappears many times during the entrepreneurial journey. You are at all times juggling real plans in an abstract context.

Still, with Mr Lindop's blessing we had completed our first, and perhaps most critical, sale. Coffee Republic was ready to leave the drawing board and look for its feet in the real world. It was more than us alone, and more than our idea.

In raising money, we utilised all the skills we had learned on the entrepreneurial road to that point (enthusiasm, dedication, energy, commitment). Balance sheets and spreadsheets, we discovered, may be the language of business but it's your personality that brings the words to life and ensures that you will succeed.

FACSIMILE 27 MARCH: 2.00PM

CHAPTER SIX:
IMPLEMENTATION
TURNING THE IDEA INTO A BUSINESS

If you think raising money for a start-up is difficult, then try finding suppliers! Even though
- you've got the great idea,
- you've written a great business plan,
- you've perfected your sales pitch,
- you've half killed yourself trying to raise money,
- you now have that money in the bank,

...the truth is you're still not an entrepreneur. The most important challenge before you become an entrepreneur now stands in your path: you have to translate all your great strategies into concrete decisions and actions that will actually build a business. Turning paper into bricks and mortar, as it were. This is the implementation phase.

Law 37: The success of your idea depends on the quality of your implementation

For us, this meant opening our first coffee bar. Alarmingly, when many would-be entrepreneurs reach this stage, they are labouring under the mistaken impression that the hard work is done. This is a particularly common trap for MBA-trained entrepreneurs. They think that somehow, because they've completed the strategic stage (the great business plan, the financing, etc.), that the rest will take care of itself. It won't. Implementation is as important as the strategy formulation. And the QUALITY of the implementation matters at least as much as and sometimes more than the formulation of a strategy.

THAT'S EXACTLY WHY YOU HAVE TO IMPLEMENT YOUR BUSINESS PLAN YOURSELF, AND NOT LEAVE IT TO SOMEONE ELSE.

Implementing your business plan is NOT the easy bit! Implementation is the point at which you really find out, as an entrepreneur, what you're made of.

"The image of the entrepreneur as a great inventor and great promoter or the great and daring risk taker simply doesn't square with the facts. Reality is far less spectacular than this. In fact in the beginning entrepreneurship turns out to be a mundane affair and not at all heroic. There is the entrepreneur without capital source, without apparent social skills and without an even good idea. No respectable element in the community is even aware of him, let alone ready to help him."
- LAWRENCE STEINMETZ

What, then, defines a successful entrepreneur? Do you think it's the quality of the initial research? Or perhaps the thoroughness of the business plan? Or the long-term audacious goals that have been set? Or do you suspect that it could be how effectively funds were raised, and how much capital the business has at its disposal? The answer is none of the above! The successful entrepreneur is the one who rolls up his sleeves and gets his hands dirty; who personally attends to every last, minor detail that affects the business.

There is a good analogy about climbing Everest to demonstrate the difference between implementation and strategy (i.e. what you've done so far).

"A typical business strategy resembles a map of Everest. Getting to the top of Everest is challenging not because of the scarcity of reliable maps but because of the difficulty of the climb. Reaching the summit requires in addition to a reliable map, exceptional determination, endurance and an ability to make judgments under difficult conditions."

- AMAR BHIDE, The Origin and Evolution of New Businesses

In the same way while your business plan and vision help direct your effort, actually building your business successfully requires a capacity to execute that strategy. Here are the reasons for the importance of implementation and why you have to execute your idea yourself:

Law 38: The quality of your implementation is what will set you apart from the competition

That's something that no one can copy! If you think about it, anyone can copy your strategy. You invariably end up sharing your concept with a lot of people and so it can easily fall into the hands of rivals. Assuming these rivals broadly follow the same strategy, then your success will largely be determined by the quality of your implementation.

We entered a business where barriers to entry were very low. Anyone could copy our coffee menu, our takeaway cups or even our design (and many did). But what really set us apart was that we delivered what we set out to deliver consistently at every customer experience. Thus, our only real barriers to entry lay in the quality of our implementation. Quality implementation is the safest insurance you can have against potential rivals because no one can copy the quality of your own uniquely individual approach!

Law 39: You are still swimming against the tide

Remember the commitment and determination you needed to get through the minefield of doubts, obstacles and nay-sayers, first with yourself, then your friends, then your bankers. Well, it gets even worse at the implementation stage with all the people that you are hoping will support your business: suppliers, retail agents, employees, designers, architects. You might think that with a great potential idea and a cheque book in hand that these people will be vying for your attention. Wrong!

Your plans will be greeted with a considerable degree of scepticism by all the forces within the market that exist already. Innovators by definition shake up the established order, and no established order ever thinks that it is in need of a shake-up. You'll need to grow a thick skin too because, if you're lucky, a lot of people will tell you that you're idea isn't going to work. If you're unlucky, they'll be more blunt and simply tell you that your idea is stupid. The extraordinary paradox is that these are people who would have an enormous vested interest if your business worked.

One supplier we remember serenaded us with sob stories about other failed coffee entrepreneurs (instead of giving us a presentation of his machines). Having been immersed in two hours of constant discouragement from him, we both felt like throwing ourselves off London Bridge, conveniently located next door to his showroom.

We remember sitting in front of coffee suppliers (what's in it for them?) who would go out of their way to persuade us how wrong we were and how coffee bars would never work. In fact, coffee suppliers were the most demoralising of them all. Their attitude was truly baffling!

The only person who can navigate safely through these largely uncharted and very choppy waters is YOU. You'll be seen as 'unconventional' and it will be up to you to muster the determination and focus you'll need to keep things moving ahead. You can imagine how, if you simply hired someone to do the legwork for you, they might never make it through the barriers and obstacles that they would find in their way. This sort of resistance needs strong doses of entrepreneurial persistence and determination to overcome.

If you have any doubts, then you'll find history littered with examples of people that we now accept as geniuses (in business or otherwise) and products that we today consider invaluable, all of which had to overcome initial rejection. Post-It notes were originally deemed to be totally worthless. Paul McCartney was refused entry to his school choir. The list goes on.

Law 40: The resources won't be there so YOU have to fill the gap between what's out there and what you need

If you're entering an untapped market and therefore doing something that's by definition innovative, then you need to remember that the support network of suppliers and resources you'll eventually come to rely on may not exist at the start or, if it does exist, it might not be in the form that you ideally need. This is actually no bad thing; if your business simply slipped easily into an existing framework of suppliers and resources, then you'd probably start wondering if you were offering something different at all! Alarm bells should start ringing if, when you enter, suppliers and information are ready and waiting for you. That would mean someone must be using your idea already.

In short, your idea is new and different, but existing supply chains offer only the old and the established so you will need to be resourceful in filling the gap between what's out there and what you need. Creativity comes into play here, and that is a key entrepreneurial characteristic. Thinking outside the box, being persistent, being persuasive: these are the tools that, as a pioneering entrepreneur, you have to deploy.

For example, we found that although there was a strong network of suppliers of coffee beans, coffee machines and other key materials, they didn't supply the specific quality we were looking for which made life difficult for us. For example, for coffee making itself, while our concept required special milk thermometers, special foaming jugs, foaming spoons, etc., the industry was just used to using 'any old jug' and nothing else. So we had to order all our coffee making accessories by FedEx from a US mail order catalogue, which was very impractical indeed!

You might think that at least we had coffee machines. We didn't. The coffee machines were built for those squatty china cups and didn't fit our grande and tall paper cup sizes. These were too tall to fit under the espresso pourers. Although the great Italian brands later reluctantly built (through gritted teeth) special tall machines for the new style coffee bars, we had to laboriously make do with a complicated system of pouring espresso into shot glasses, and only then into our own cups.

We found that with almost everything we looked for, either it wasn't available or it wasn't of the quality we needed, so we always had to come up with a creative solution.

Law 41: Credibility has to be EARNED.
You have a 'liability of newness'

Credibility doesn't grow on trees and respect has to be earned by you. Even if you find suppliers and others who believe in your idea, the fact is that to them you're still an unknown quantity with no track record.

While investors and bankers may judge you on a combination of your business plan and how compelling you are as an individual, your resource providers in the implementation world (like suppliers, employees, and agents) need proof that they will be paid. They need to know that you can meet your bills – and you have no way of proving it.

You can get around this hurdle but the only way you can persuade them to take a chance on your start-up is by using all the entrepreneurial qualities that you have used before to get you this far. You will have to be at your most persuasive and compelling, because the people you are trying to convince are, essentially, being asked to risk their own money by partnering with you (which is effectively what a supplier does). They face considerable risks dealing with you and you can show them no credible proof of your staying power. Therefore you have to be imaginative and think out of the box. And let's face it; no one is more likely to be successful in getting people on board than you.

We pulled out all the stops to get resource providers to do business with us. We interviewed many until we found the right fit. Some went with us because they were entrepreneurial themselves. Others wanted the kudos of helping a start-up. Some took a risk on us as individuals, others because they needed the business, and any business would do! However it was, we managed somehow or other.

Law 42: The devil is in the detail

As an entrepreneur, be warned that the following phrase no longer exists: 'It's only a minor detail.'

Forget you've ever heard those words. There is NO SUCH THING as a minor detail, and no such thing as a detail that is unimportant, a detail that can be overlooked, or a detail that can be left for a rainy day.

Everyone thinks of entrepreneurs as 'big picture' people and that is probably fair. All entrepreneurs do see the big picture, because that's where the process of entrepreneurship starts. However, successful entrepreneurs are also 'little picture' people, too. They have tapped into the value of the phrase 'it's all in the detail'.

Think about it this way: What is your brand? Is it an idea that you dreamed up in bed one night? No, it's not. Your brand is what you did with that idea. It is the sum total of every single step, the big ones and tiny ones, that you've taken to turn the dream into a reality. The constituent parts of a brand are a million and one details that, together, form the message that you are trying to convey. Would you trust someone else to take responsibility for those details? If you did, you'd be putting the crucial task of building your brand into someone else's hands. That's why in beginning you have to do it ALL yourself.

If it's any consolation, Sam Walton of Walmart chose the first 130 stores and until Walmart grew to 500 stores he continued to keep up with every real estate deal made. Bill Gates still reportedly reviews the code that programmers at Microsoft write. Retail is detail no matter whether you are a multibillion-dollar powerhouse or an embryonic start-up!

In our case, we were well aware that every last facet of our first store would give a message about the Coffee Republic brand. So together we chose every plate, every chair, every napkin... everything. With each, no matter how trivial the purchase seemed we asked ourselves "What message does this give out about our brand?" Many times we found ourselves in the middle of Heals, Habitat or John Lewis kitchen departments arguing about which cake plate was 'Coffee Republic' and which was 'un-Coffee Republic'.

To give an example that forever sticks in our minds, we searched high and low for a 'push/pull' sign for our door. We couldn't afford a branded one, but we didn't want a stock brass sign because those are so redolent of the old-style sandwich bars that we wanted to supplant. Spending hours on such a decision shows exactly what we mean by being committed to every last detail in your business. In the end, even our 'push/pull' sign did give out a brand message, so it had to be the right one.

Law 43: The bootstrapping rule. 2+2 = 5

A LESSON FROM SAHAR:

I will never forget the shock when I started my two years of training in the law firm I had always dreamed of working for. I was all excited, all suited up to get my training to be a fully-fledged lawyer. Do you know what I spent most of my time doing? Photocopying and proofreading!

The benefit of these boring duties for a well-paid trainee lawyer completely eluded me, especially when in the big law firms there were enough staff in the photocopy departments to get that sort of work done. It was not until two years into Coffee Republic that I finally understood why I'd been made to do it.

Here's why: by getting a trainee lawyer to start doing the menial tasks you are teaching them what it takes to work in the law from the ground up. You are teaching them the nuts and bolts of working in a firm, and the process required to craft a document from start to finish. Thus the trainee is not getting lazy by simply relying on knowledge acquired through years of studying. Being a lawyer is about 'doing' as well as 'knowing'.

This is called BOOTSTRAPPING.

The Oxford English Dictionary defines bootstrapping as an activity 'carried out with minimum resources or advantages.' Conventionally it's associated with economising and saving pennies, but we think the real definition is wider than that. The real benefit of bootstrapping comes from the discipline that lack of money brings to entrepreneurs. It forces them to make two plus two equal five and to use what they have in the most resourceful and productive manner. As they do this, they learn to be a business and act in a business-like way.

So bootstrapping is a discipline to impose on yourself. It will teach you to be resourceful and to focus on targeting customer needs. By doing so, by relying on your own hard work and nothing else, your individual focus will become laser sharp.

Almost all great entrepreneurs started off by bootstrapping. Try and take the easy way and...well, here's an example. The exact opposite of bootstrapping is what a lot of the dot.coms did during the Internet boom. Because investors were falling over themselves to jump on the bandwagon, money was literally being thrown at start-ups who barely had to justify their business plans. New companies found themselves with as much money as they needed for lavish offices, enormous advertising and marketing budgets and bloated staff rolls, without ever having to learn much about their actual businesses.

Guess what happened? Having all that money caused them to think in an unbusiness-like way. It cushioned them from having to learn their customers' needs and from adapting their businesses to best meet those needs in the most efficient and productive manner possible. The Internet boomers thus lost touch with their creations, with little personal drive behind many of the companies and with money being used as a poor substitute for creativity.

All of this was, of course, avoidable. And no matter how successful you may be in terms of funding, it provides a salutary lesson for budding entrepreneurs to learn. Do NOT avoid bootstrapping. Start in the mailroom, even if you own the business. Work your way up. Put in the effort, and the rewards will be there. Even on the traditional corporate ladder, numerous top executives have worked their way from the ground floor up, and it has paid off. Every entrepreneur should follow in these footsteps. If your business does well, you won't be on the ground floor for long.

IMPLEMENTATION: How any one can do it

Using the Everest analogy, if implementation is actually climbing Everest then you are now at Base Camp and the summit is miles away. How do you get there? Don't be alarmed. There is a secret to it. Bobby's favourite analogy is that you can eat an elephant if you approach it one bite at a time. That is the secret to doing anything you want in life. It is also the secret to implementation:

Law 44: You can do anything, no matter how monumental, if you break it down into small, manageable chunks

Ask a mountain climber how to scale Everest, and you'll find they don't just set off and stroll upwards until they get to the summit. In fact, it takes about three months of elapsed time to summit the world's highest mountain and it's an exercise not just in physical fortitude but also in planning, organisation and detail. There are, in fact, five separate camps between Base Camp and the top of the mountain, and reaching each of these is a victory in itself.

You start a business in the same way. You don't do it overnight; in fact, you don't even try to. So don't worry about the size of the task, just break it into small, manageable pieces and keep your momentum moving in the right direction this way. Before you know it, you'll be looking down from the summit of your original goal.

To make it clearer and stick with the mountain analogy, Base Camp is where your original idea resides. To get onto the mountain itself and towards camp one, write out a comprehensive, thorough, all encompassing to-do list of every single item (and we mean every!) that you need to do in order to start your business. It should start the day you write it and end the day your business becomes operational.

Once you've done your to-do list, go through it and prioritise the tasks in order of urgency and/or importance. You're on the way to Camp Two. There you'll find what in business terms is called CRITICAL PATH ANALYSIS. Because of all the many things you need to do, you may veer off track and this analysis is really a list to keep you on the critical path. And so it goes until, in time, you do reach the top of the mountain. As you can imagine, your to-do list will be substantial. And whilst every last item is your own responsibility, you need to understand that you won't be able to do everything at once. This means that you have to prioritise. You have to know and be able to distinguish between the details which are not worth getting bogged down in, and those which need your immediate attention. The process of working this out entails time management.

The key to good time management is to focus attention away from 'urgent' issues and to proactively work on important things which may be, but are not necessarily, urgent instead. It is the important things that make a difference, and enable us to seize the opportunities ahead of us.

HOW do you not lose sight of the forest for the trees? Taking the above rule into account (focusing on what is important, even if it's not urgent), how do you decide what the key priorities actually are?

We think that they are usually those things that are the essence of your brand, your unique selling points (USPs), what differentiates you from your competition. If you were to stand for one word, what would it be? These are items that must be handled quickly and effectively because they lie at the core of your product or service offer.

OUR PRIORITIES IN GETTING COFFEE REPUBLIC GOING
March 1995

1. Form limited company

2. Find a retail site

3. Get the coffee right

4. Shop fitting

5. Logo

Our Story: implementation:
March 1995 — November 1995

By end of March 1995, as you know, we had raised the money we needed. So the time had finally come where we were in position to take the plunge and open our first store. Although an immense amount of work still had to be done, at this stage our feelings were primarily those of relief because we knew that at last we could actually start taking action, rather than simply talking about going ahead with our idea. At this point, our first store was firmly on the horizon.

Our research stage had given us a pretty good idea of what we would do when this point arrived. We had, you'll remember, met lots of suppliers, looked at the equipment that we would need and familiarised ourselves with everything involved in opening our doors for the first time. When we did the research, of course, we had no funding so at the time we were not sure whether we'd able to go ahead. However, in our mind's eye, we had a pretty clear idea even then whom we wanted to work with and how we wanted our business to look once the money had been raised. Thus, with the funding secured, we were in position to move quickly on a number of fronts.

With our cheque book in hand, we were suddenly running a real business! So the next challenge was actually a physical one, ordering and installing all the equipment and products that we had chosen. You might think that we were now entering the exciting stage, but we were surprised to find ourselves confronted by an unexpected problem. We knew our business was now credible, but suppliers simply didn't see it that way! No one seemed prepared to take us seriously.

A good example of the scepticism that we faced was the attitude of the company we wanted to supply our coffee machines. We knew exactly what brand of machine we wanted so when we went to see the distributors, we were very enthusiastic. We told them that we loved their machines and we specified what we were interested in down to the last detail.

In turn the supplier also got very excited about our proposal launch and helped us with various other things and contacts that we needed. We even did all our coffee tastings in their showrooms. But then we got busy with the business plan and raising money so we lost touch with these people for a couple of months. When we finally called them to really order the machine about which we'd enthused for so long, the first thing the rep said to Sahar on picking up the phone was "There was a bet at the office whether you'd be back or not. I said that you wouldn't come back, that you didn't look like you were serious about it." He then said "It looks like I've lost the bet." He definitely had, and as he has since supplied 150 of his coffee machines to Coffee Republic, he probably doesn't mind too much!

Remember the general rules we told you about how difficult and challenging it is for entrepreneurs to find suppliers, employees and other resource providers. Well just listen to our adventures below...

CHALLENGE ONE – *Finding a site*
Here is our story. We received the letter from NatWest agreeing to lend us the money we needed to set up Coffee Republic in April 1995. But we didn't open our first store until the 4 November that year. That's seven months later. What took us so long?

The answer is finding a site.

In truth, we probably vastly underestimated just how difficult this challenge would be. As a retail business, we knew that the old adage of 'location, location, location' was going to be critical. Our site selection strategy was to identify high traffic, high visibility locations in densely populated office areas so that we could attract a loyal base of customers who would come in to our shop daily, and hopefully more than once a day.

However, we had no idea how the commercial property market worked. We tried to educate ourselves by talking to everyone we knew in that field and by chasing any leads we were given. We started by meeting surveyors whom friends recommended to us, and after that we called others we'd found in the Yellow Pages. We even had a 'surveyors week' when we must have met about 20 different companies, giving each of them a full presentation on our concept. We were so tired by the end that we had fits of giggles launching into the same story time and time again.

All the surveyors that we met appeared enthusiastic and promised to call us back. But most of them never bothered to do so. They would hardly even return our calls to them. Remember the rule: Entrepreneurs have no credibility!

We soon learned that those in the property field saw us with the same lack of belief as our suppliers. And this was compounded by a further problem, that great sites never come on the property market. Instead they change hands between agents way before businesses like ours ever hear about them. So as a newcomer you need the best and most experienced agent possible on your side. Yet the best ones will have no time for you, because they have bigger fish to fry.

In short, you find yourself trapped in a vicious circle and only one thing, a true entrepreneurial quality, is going to get you out: determination. We were not going to lose our dream because those we needed to help us succeed were not as committed as we were. So we set about proving to the world of surveyors that we were going to make things happen for Coffee Republic.

How did we do this? We picked a surveyor that we thought was the best and most experienced: Colin Baxter of Blanchflower Lloyd

Baxter. To this day we remind Colin (who has found about 60 sites for Coffee Republic) that he made us wait 45 minutes outside his office at our first meeting, and that he essentially didn't give us the time of day.

We bombarded – and we're not exaggerating – Colin with our determination to find a site. We called him every day, twice a day at least. If he told us about sites, we would immediately get into the car, visit the site and within minutes report back. We practically forced meetings on him. We were so keen that even if a site was nothing more than a slight possibility, we would do our homework on it so as to give the agents no excuses for not taking us equally seriously.

We now put our determination down to the wonderful naivety that the enthusiasm behind entrepreneurship brings with it. We did endless pavement counts on sites that we had only a small chance of getting. We spent hours outside prospective stores counting the number of people passing by at various times of day. This would give us an idea of the number of customers we could expect. Since Sahar insisted on doing the counting from the comfort of her car, inevitably parked on a yellow line, the counting process was disturbed many a time by the need to fend off traffic wardens – such are the challenges of pursuing a dream!

Having done the counting and homework we would get very excited at the prospect of a future site, usually then to be rejected by landlords. Landlords are reluctant to lease premises to new businesses with no track record and we had the added hurdle that ours was an unfamiliar concept for them, let alone an unfamiliar name. They could not grasp that we would really be different from traditional cafes and sandwich bars.

And so our challenge continued.

A cartoon drawn by Bobby of Sahar looking for sites

As the days passed, it seemed to us that the coffee boom from the US was slowly gathering pace in the UK market. Endless rumours were reaching our ears; everyone we spoke to in the industry seemed to know someone who was planning to start a coffee chain in London.

Most of this was just scaremongering but it worked in putting fuel into our already revved up engines. We wanted to be the first to market and the first in customers' minds. On our daily knowledge trips around London we would carefully survey every shop that had just closed or was under construction to make sure that no competitors were opening.

If all of this sounds like determination bordering on paranoia, we can go back to the mountain analogy again. Planning and dedication are everything. If you're going to climb Everest, remember that you won't get the job done by simply walking up the hill. There's no point getting five hundred yards from the summit, only to find out you've run out of rope. You have to check and investigate every last facet of your business or expedition, and then when you're satisfied that you have overlooked nothing you have to check again.

...and then, our first competitor appeared!
The day before Good Friday, we saw the one thing that we desperately did not want to see. A window poster on a site in Long Acre in Covent Garden announced: "Double Vanilla Skinny Latte arrives in Covent Garden." A company called the Seattle Coffee Company was going to open before us – and judging by the language in their poster, they were arriving with exactly the same idea!

When we saw the poster, we were speechless. It was obvious from their branding that they were as serious we were. However, after our initial panic was over, we decided that having a competitor was a fact of business life. And actually, it might even be a good thing since our concept was so new it would help educate the market more quickly into the joys of gourmet coffee.

In the event, until they sold out to Starbucks three years later, they were our only serious competitor.

To be honest, at that time we were getting quite demoralised. By July, we had not yet found a site despite establishing a close relationship with our surveyors and also spending every minute of the day in our car (without air conditioning) in the summer heat, looking for locations.

FACSIMILE (FROM BOBBY TO SAHAR)

Can't help feeling out of steam – We have been trying for five months and nothing closed yet!

We were also under increasing pressure from NatWest, whose loan was conditional on us finding a site. It was becoming difficult to sustain the enthusiasm of bankers, suppliers and advisers for such an extended period of time, particularly when our own credibility was far from established. But that's the entrepreneurial life, always a matter of juggling, and wondering whether the chicken or the egg comes first.

Finally in July, and quite by chance, we got a well-deserved lucky break on sites. One morning Sahar bumped into an old friend and was moaning to him about the difficulties we faced finding our first site. Trying to be helpful, Simon mentioned that a friend of his had a luxury T-shirt shop on South Molton Street, and might be keen to exit his lease.

Law 45: Success happens when preparation meets opportunity

We had prepared for eight months for this opportunity and we were not going to let it go. Sahar immediately drove to South Molton Street and saw the store. We had already done a lot of homework and a pavement count for the site opposite so we knew it was the right profile for us.

And there it was. At 8.30 a.m. on a beautiful July morning, Coffee Republic had found its first site.

The great thing about this was that because we had got an inside tip, we were able to 'beat the market'. We set Colin on to it immediately. Even better, we got quite a good deal on the site. Remember that in 1995 property prices had not yet recovered from the early 90s slump, so we got away with a small premium and nice rent-free period.

South Molton Street was ideal for Coffee Republic's first store as it offered a combination of all the customer bases we had targeted. It had a full cross-section of office workers, shoppers, commuters, students and tourists. We were also hoping that with Condé Nast (home of Vogue, GQ, Tatler etc.) round the corner, we would attract attention from the press. As South Molton Street was pedestrianised, we had the added bonus of outside seating which we needed, given that the store was 245 sq. ft.

With hindsight we were very lucky to find the location, though maybe it was our hard work and persistence that made us lucky. Either way, South Molton Street was a fantastic first site. It was the ideal pilot store. We finally signed the lease in August. But from July, since we had signed heads of terms, we had the certainty of a site and could thus proceed confidently with the rest of items on our lengthy to-do list.

We were a major step closer to realising our dream!

CHALLENGE TWO – Finding the suppliers
We thought from the start that the key to success lay in the coffee itself. We knew that unless we served great quality coffee that there

was no point going into business. We thus had to aim for the very highest quality available on the market.

The problem was that, in real terms, we knew nothing about coffee at all.

The first thing we did during our research stage was, as we said, earlier, to become 'Zulus' about coffee. By going to meet all the suppliers, attending all the training courses, reading all the books and literature, we taught ourselves everything there was to know about how coffee is grown, the different beans, and the different blends. So we were armed with vital knowledge before we set out to find the supplier who would supply us with the right blend of coffee for Coffee Republic.

This is an important point. What we did was to learn about coffee before we needed to make purchasing decisions, so the learning process could be objective and independent of an immediate commercial need. At that stage there was no pressure on us to choose a coffee, only to learn about what we would later be buying.

Thus, in time we were expert enough to identify the blend of coffee we believed that we were looking for. That was Sahar's speciality. In her months of research and coffee tasting she had identified certain key characteristics she wanted in a typical latte or espresso. She wanted the coffee to be strong, to have a 'good kick', but without having a bitter aftertaste.

We remember how shocked suppliers were when we told them our specifications. They would say "That's a great blend" or "That's superior quality" and Sahar would stubbornly answer that as a Latte it didn't have the kick or the flavour she was looking for. We were surprised that coffee suppliers actually didn't bend over backwards for our business. We thought that once we had a cheque book in hand, they would compete vigorously to get our business and do everything possible to supply us with exactly what we needed.

Instead, most of the suppliers said, "This is what we have and if it's not good enough for you then you're wrong and you can go somewhere else." We found the big coffee suppliers had established systems and methods of doing things that had worked well for them over the years and our new demands and extra pickiness were thought to be just an unnecessary inconvenience. They almost couldn't be bothered to deal with us. Most of the others thought we were crazy to do a coffee bar chain at all! (Remember the rule about swimming against the tide.)

We soon learned that what we needed were suppliers who were entrepreneurial and thought like us. Suppliers who believed in our vision and would thus take a chance on going the extra mile to meet our needs. In the event, there was only one supplier who seemed to feel that way. She ran the London branch of a small family roastery in Italy and we met her at a trade fair. She stood out because she was the only supplier who was willing to listen to Sahar's passion about the exact taste she was looking for in a blend. She got us to try so many blends and she never gave up if things weren't quite right. That is why, in the end, she won the Coffee Republic business. Her passion and determination matched our own.

One day Sahar got a call from her saying "Can you meet me at Oriel in Sloane Square in 20 minutes? I think I've found the blend you want." Sahar turned up at Oriel, had a sip of the proposed coffee, and there she found exactly the rich taste that she had been searching for all along. That day the Coffee Republic blend was born. The blend we chose together went on to win many awards including the Best Cappuccino in London by the Independent on Sunday and Best Espresso in London by the Guardian.

With hindsight we can now see how important it was that the supplier of our most important raw material was as passionate and committed as we were to our dream. Eva was invaluable source of help and support throughout. She became like a partner with us in the growth of Coffee Republic. She was there with us personally at each of our store openings. She was in essence a bootstrapper herself and as such she was exactly what we needed. Having got her on board we then focused on getting the right coffee making equipment. In Italy they say that the secret to great coffee is the 5Ms:

- Mescla – the blend of coffee,
- Machina – the quality of the coffee machine,
- Machinadosatore – the grinder, which grinds the coffee beans,
- Mesura – the grams of coffee used per espresso shot, and
- Mano – the hand of the espresso operator.

Our next task was to get the rest of the 5Ms right!

We knew exactly what type of machine and grinder we wanted. From our research we had found out that different machines affect the taste of espresso so from our tastings we had identified the brand that produced the taste that we wanted for Coffee Republic. It was the Italian Cimbali machine, and it happened to be the most expensive on the market. We remember that even coffee machine suppliers were surprised that we were so set on exactly what we wanted, and that nothing else would do. But this is the sort of perfectionism that makes the difference between success and failure for an entrepreneur.

One inspiring and amusing story we learned early on was how coffee was discovered.

Legend has it that in the early sixth century in Ethiopia there was a goat herder called Kaldi. One day, Kaldi noticed that when he took his goats to a particular mountaintop, which had tall plants with bright red berries, his goats were particularly chirpy and energetic. So he picked a couple of the red berries and took them to the local sage to solve the puzzle.

The local sage, having had enough of villagers claiming magic, took the berries in anger from Kaldi and threw them into the fire. The berries in the fire started roasting and giving off an intoxicating aroma of freshly roasted coffee... the local sage was smitten and the rest is history.

We loved this story so much we even considered calling our concept Kaldi's Coffee!

CHALLENGE THREE – *Finding the right food suppliers*

With the coffee issues resolved, we next had to move on to food. Here, we found it very difficult sourcing suppliers for the things that we wanted to serve. A big part of our coffee experience was the delicious offer of foods that we had seen in New York: fat-free blueberry muffins, oatmeal cookies, biscotti, double chocolate brownies, and so on.

The food quality in sandwich bars at that time was totally lacklustre and poor. Thus suppliers that baked the type of gourmet pastries we were looking for simply didn't exist.

When we spoke to the suppliers we could find, we might as well have been speaking a different language. They simply could not grasp our beliefs when it came to things like quality, presentation, attitude and customer satisfaction. It became very obvious that for food as well as coffee, we were really bringing a whole new culture, a different mindset, to the market.

Wholesale suppliers that had been around for years were closed to any possibility of changing their systems, methods and recipes as these had been firmly established and had worked well for them so far. Knowing then that we could not rely on the usual pool of suppliers, we had to be more imaginative and basically turn to bootstrapping once again.

For our muffins, we bought a muffin recipe book in New York. With the recipes in hand, we needed someone to cook them for us and deliver them to the shop every day. Back then the only place that served gourmet cakes like courgette and poppy seed was Joseph's Café on Sloane Street. They also had a delicious dessert called 'Delice au Café' which was really heaven on earth. We found out that the same person made the cakes and desserts for Joseph's and with a few phone calls we found out her details. We thought if she could concoct the 'Delice au café', she could definitely make the muffins for Coffee Republic!

Taking this step broke all the rules Bobby had set in terms of suppliers. Not only was this lady not big, commercial, with national distribution, etc., she wasn't even really a proper supplier. Her only client was Joseph, to which she delivered a few desserts every week. But she could deliver the quality and choice we needed to have, so we went with her.

We had the same story with French pastries (croissants, pain au chocolats). The quality of the big suppliers was not good enough for Coffee Republic and the only croissant that met our standard was one from a shop called St Quentin in Knightsbridge. They also made the most authentic French baguette sandwiches. But they never did wholesale and they had no delivery system in place.

Here, we took the view that what was important was getting the quality right for opening and other details could be resolved later. So since we could not afford to hire a van, we decided to do deliveries ourselves for the first couple of months. At least St Quentin was halfway between our house and our South Molton Street shop.

Bagels were a bit of an embarrassing story. Sahar insisted that the Brick Lane bagels were the best in London and Coffee Republic had to have them. Nothing else would do. Anyone familiar with the Brick Lane bagel shop will know that however great and authentic the goods are, 'professional' is not a word you'd use to describe the supplier!

Our solution was to find a black cabbie who lived in the East End and who would pick them up at Brick Lane at the crack of dawn, on his way into the West End. The problem we soon found was that with his cab fare included the bagels cost more than we sold them for. So we found a decent bagel store on the Fulham Road and decided to pick them up ourselves every morning!

Once again, a combination of inspiration, perspiration and determination proved to be the order of the day.

CHALLENGE FOUR – *Building a brand:*
We had set out to build the leading brand of espresso bars in the UK. Yet, quite apart from the logistical problems addressed already, we also knew nothing about marketing or branding.

Law 46: There is a lot to be said for the naivety of entrepreneurs. The importance of being clueless

Thinking back on it, we did not let ourselves be intimidated by branding. We did not allow ourselves to be constrained by our total lack of experience in an area people were typically highly trained in. For us, branding was simply the message that Coffee Republic would give to customers about itself and this was something that was not hard to grasp. We knew we wouldn't be there to explain to each customer everything that we stood for, so the brand needed to do the job for us. It would speak on our behalf to the outside world.

We would communicate our brand message to customers firstly through the store design (the store would technically act like a billboard), and secondly through every single item inside the store (the type of cups, choices of sugar, the thickness of the napkins, the baristas' uniforms, etc.).

In terms of the look of Coffee Republic, our store shop fitting and design was something we had to decide on quickly as the costs were the biggest start-up expense we had and it was going to take some time to achieve what we wanted.

The challenge for us was that we were both totally clueless about the issues that we were facing. We didn't know much about decorating houses, let alone shops. We didn't even know who designed shops: was it architects, shop fitters, decorators, or another party altogether? Now, of course, we know that there are companies specialising in retail design, but we had no idea then. Being complete novices, we were deprived of a host of valuable information we only discovered later.

We did some asking around and people suggested that we hire architects. We had no idea which firm to hire so someone recommended that we visit various shops and restaurants and pinpoint those that we liked and find out who designed them. We quite liked the Jigsaw on High Street Kensington, and also the Joseph stores. We called their head offices and after some additional investigation we discovered they had been designed by Nigel Coates and Eva Jiricna respectively.

We approached each of these two world famous architects (not knowing quite how famous they were; they have both been involved in architectural landmarks around the world) to design our 245 sq. ft. coffee bar.

We can now put it down to entrepreneurial naivety that we approached these two to design a coffee bar on a very tight budget and – to add insult to injury – we knew exactly how we wanted the bar to look. As we had photos from New York, we needed no creativity; all we needed was for someone to copy themes from our New York photos and the sketches we had visualised.

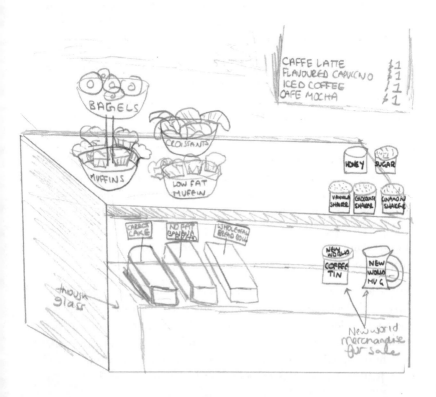

In the end, we went with Eva Jiricna. We spent hours on every single detail of the shop fitting. With hindsight we now know what a star she was to take so graciously what amounted to us telling a world expert how to do her job!

The next key challenge was designing our logo. As part of our branding we wanted everything inside the store to have our badge on it, from cups, napkins and bags to the employees' uniforms.

We had a budget of £400 to design the logo, and yet again we had no idea where to turn to find a designer. At first we asked a friend who worked for a big brand identity company that only big multinationals could afford whether she could help. Her solution was to get one of the agency's top designers to design our logo under a sort of moonlighting arrangement.

This proved to be a disaster. Similar to the situation with the architects, we didn't need a creative genius; we just needed a designer to draw what we couldn't draw but could envision ourselves. When you are inexperienced you don't really have the confidence to say 'no' without feeling guilty. So we would meet this genius designer after hours and be at pains to reject his designs politely. He would be insulted as he hardly ever had his work turned back. We would feel awkward and unfair, especially as we knew his firm would have charged tens of thousands for his work.

But our instinct told us that however stubborn and unreasonable we may have appeared, we had to be true to the soul of the business we had in our hearts. And however gifted or experienced advisers were, they would not bully us into accepting what we felt did not capture our dreams.

We finally parted ways with the genius designer and basically walked away from the talent of the UK's top corporate identity agency in the process. Instead, we found a small graphic designer our architects recommended who would produce what we wanted.

Once we had the logo we could go ahead and order our packaging and uniforms. But since we had already spent our £400 budget on the first failed attempt, we had no more money left for design and so ended up once more bootstrapping a lot of what needed to be done.

For example, we couldn't afford to order cups printed with our logo, so our solution was to order stickers and stick them on white cups ourselves. At nights we would sit in front of the TV and ask friends round for an evening at which all of us would stick stickers on cups!

We ended up designing leaflets ourselves, as we couldn't afford to get the graphic designer to do the work. Since we weren't very confident about our ability to write persuasive prose for customer brochures, we got a great friend of ours, Mariella (who is extremely witty) to come round to dinner and help us to write it. Thus one September night we came up with the necessary goods over a plate of pasta and a bottle of red wine.

CHALLENGE FIVE – *Finding employees.*

Finding people to work for us was another venture into unknown territory. That said we were absolutely sure about the importance of providing superior customer service from the outset. We needed employees who were clean and fresh, extremely friendly looking, and very enthusiastic about our great coffee offer. These were the people who would introduce customers to the variety of custom made coffee drinks that were the key to our business success.

We made the following cartoon to really personify the type of customer service we were envisaging.

The next thing we did was to put an advert in the Evening Standard on a Tuesday because we were told that this was what everyone in catering did.

The next day we were inundated with over 100 phone calls from prospective employees who had worked in the sort of establishments that provided the mediocre customer service we

wanted to distinguish ourselves from. We were attracting exactly the calibre of staff that represented what we didn't want to be.

Once again, we found the gulf between what is available and what you want. Our other problem was that once we had secured employees, we had no skills or means of training them.

Guess how we got around the problem? We bootstrapped! We decided that since we had no idea how to train employees, our only solution was to hire employees that were ready trained.

The only customer service we respected at the time was Pret A Manger's. They had been the first to alter the standards of customer service in the industry in the UK. Their employees were uniformed, clean and unbelievably enthusiastic and helpful. We figured that if we got our first employees from Pret we would not need to train them. They would be ready trained, and immediately Coffee Republic would – by osmosis – provide the same levels of customer service as Pret! Put it down to naivety again – the importance of being clueless!

To be honest, we set about poaching two employees from Pret. We printed little strips with our name and number and headed off to the Pret A Manger in St Martins Lane. This was their biggest store, so we figured that we would be less conspicuous in its busy environment. If you have ever approached unsuspecting employees with a job offer you will understand exactly how ridiculous we felt.

We procrastinated, got cold feet, left and returned, pushed each other forward, until finally we gathered the courage to approach one employee who was packing egg mayo sandwiches onto one of the shelves. Although surprised by our advance, he appeared very keen. We promised a pay rise and he promised to call. His nam was Miguel and he came to see us a day later and brought another friend, Max, who was also at Pret and wanted to follow him. To cut a long and embarrassing story short we were so thrilled that they had been trained at Pret that we really did not bother to interview them. We all just agreed to meet up two days before the date of the South Molton Street opening.

Our next priority was to find a manager. We were very lucky to find a Canadian girl called Tanya who had worked in a coffee bar in the US and knew all about the preparation of the new style coffee drinks. She taught us how to make the most delicious real whipped cream (by adding a dash of vanilla) and how to make hot chocolate out of a pump dispenser, methods we still use at Coffee Republic. She did not have any experience as a manager but since we were so thrilled by her knowledge of new style coffee bars that we took her on as our manager anyway. We told her that the two hourly-paid employees she would manage were ready trained, so she would not need to worry about them.

It was not until two days before the opening of South Molton Street that having left Max and Miguel to be inducted be Tanya, we discovered that the two of them did not speak English! We had previously put down their lack of eloquence to excitement and enthusiasm and overlooked the fact that they were language students. Of course, you don't need perfect command of English to make sandwiches at Pret and pack the shelves, but you did need a good command of English to introduce Londoners to the wide choice of tailor made coffee drinks we were providing at Coffee Republic!

So Sahar spent the two days left before our grand opening accelerating their grasp of English, telling Max in particular that it was rude to say 'what?' to customers... As an entrepreneur you have to have many hats, and we had worn them all from delivery person to language teacher. As an entrepreneur you end up being simply the sum of what you need to be. A business expression is being 'chief cook and bottle washer' at the same time.

Once the priorities were done, we got down to the nitty-gritty! We have inserted our actual critical path list to prove to you the level of detail we've described, and that we had to get involved in. We knew that every item on the list below would make a real difference in our customer message, so we both laboured on every single item to get everything right.

The following list took us right through till the day of our first store opening.

As time passed we crossed more and more of these items off the to-do list with great satisfaction. And every day we saw tasks that

---

CRITICAL PATH ANALYSIS

Tuesday 1 August
1. MEETING WITH BANK
Issues to discuss re loan:
a) Timing — is government consent merely procedural?
b) Ask for capital repayment holiday of 18 months.
c) Any way we can speed up government?
d) Have we included expenses for mortgage debenture? Timing?

2. FIND CHEAP LAWYER
Questions to ask
a) Bank loan can take six weeks — is that OK?
b) Exchange on South Molton 14 August. What does that involve?
c) Can builders move in before we pay deposit?
d) At what point do we have to write cheques?
e) If I go on holiday — what day do I need to return to sign?
3. Technical
a) Solo cups from USA — take up to ten weeks to order
b) Make list of equipment to buy.

WEDNESDAY 2 AUGUST
1. Meet the architects
Issues to discuss
a) To explain to us exactly what the process involves Our input — do we have to be in daily contact — e.g. choosing chairs? How long is shop fitting?
b) Budget and cost limits by Bobby.
c) Logo — can they help us with it?
d) Can they help us find equipment?

2.EMPLOYEES
a) Find manager – ask around other coffee bars?
– Recruitment agency?
– Advert in Evening Standard, TNT, LOOT, Hotel Caterer.
b) Find baristas – hourly employees
Ask around e.g. Pret.
Place advert in TNT, Evening Standard
Contact universities – US embassy (maybe worked in US coffee bars).
Hotel Caterer (the industry magazine) has a Help Line phone number.
c) Check out pay situation
How much do we pay?
How much tax and NI?
Any legal issues with training?
d) Bonus incentives – (sounds great but how the hell do we do it) talk to an accountant. Love Starbucks' Bean options.
e) Training – how do we train our employees:
Technical i.e. operate coffee machine/make drinks.
Motivational – i.e. treat each customer enthusiastically.
f) Uniforms
T–shirt, apron, baseball cap.
Ask architects.
Personal hygiene? How can you enforce that?

3. MENU
Finalize menu ideas and PRICES

4. EQUIPMENT
a) Coffee machine
Finalize Cimbali.
Do tastings.
Make sure about training.
Delivery period.
b) Grinder
Does coffee supplier give free grinder?
Check out Cimbali. Which is the BEST?

c) Cash till
Get advice on type of till from accountants.
Check what type of tills Seattle and Pret have.
Buy or lease?
d) Display units
Ring companies in Yellow Pages.
Check all brochures we have.
Ask around. Do we buy them or build them?
e) Check whether we need:
Ice machine? (Iced coffee drinks are de rigeur)
Toaster? Love toast or is it impractical?
Fridge — how big?
f) Display equipment
Powder shakers — we MUST have all four! Cocoa, vanilla,
nutmeg, cinnamon. Can't find good one here — order from
US
Sugar shakers or sachets? Forgot what they have in NY
Cake and bagel display. Do I just go to Habitat?
Biscotti jars. Can't source them here — order from USA
e) Smaller kitchen equipment? Knives for cake cutting.
Catering shops?

5. SUPPLIES
a) Paper cups
Ones I brought back from NY are by Solo — USA?
There are no suppliers here
Order time from US 8—10 weeks
Can we print logo, or put stickers on instead?
Exactly how many do we need? No idea!
b) China cups
Do we really need them?
Washing? By hand or machine
Ask around for preferences.
c) What else do we need?
Plastic spoons/knives/forks. (Not the flimsy ones.)
Napkins. (Nice thick ones with logo.)
Water cups. (Cool idea I saw in NY.)
Bags. (With logo and nice handles — top of range.)
Orange juice cups. (With our logo.)

Paper for cakes. (Greaseproof.)
Bulk cinnamon, vanilla, nutmeg for topping. Sainsburys?

6. DRINK SUPPLIES
Find suppliers and prices for:
a) Coffee.
b) Milk. Can milkman deliver so much????
c) Orange juice. (The new freshly squeezed ones.)
d) Sugar, white and brown. Honey is de rigeur in NY!

7. FOOD PRODUCTS
a) Cakes & muffins – how many do we get? Fat free?
b) Bagels. Brick Lane is best.
c) Biscotti – no one knows what they are!
d) Croissant and morning goods. St Quentin is best but no delivery.
e) Chocolate crunch – Chocolate chip cookie.
f) Sandwiches – what type? No idea!

8. MARKETING
Design and pricing.
Loyalty cards – tenth drink free. Copy NY ones I brought back

Stamps for loyalty card – great to have CR stamp made?
Leaflets. To educate about our wide coffee choices.
Posters. To help customers order their tailor-made drinks.

10. MUSIC
Buy Stereo. Just normal one or special shop one?
Dixons? CD or tape?
Or do without music?
Must be classical/baroque/Pavarotti.

were once listed on a long list on paper transformed into a tangible achievement that was filling up the basement of South Molton Street. It was thus a joy to check out the basement every day and see our progress in the form of boxes of different shapes and sizes, which we unwrapped with more excitement than the best ever Christmas present. We loved them (not because we had at this stage gone mad!) but because it was all these little things, however trivial and mundane which together made up our new business.

We could physically see and feel our dream transformed into reality. There is nothing more satisfying than that for an entrepreneur.

CHAPTER SEVEN:
BEING IN BUSINESS
IF YOU BUILD IT, WILL THEY COME?

We had sold our idea to ourselves, then sold it to the bankers, then the suppliers. Now it was time for our biggest and most important sale of all: the sale to our customers. For a whole year we had prepared for this one final sale.

It was the night of 3 November 1995, almost exactly a year to the day after our conversation in the Thai restaurant and Coffee Republic was about to open its doors for the first time. We were about to meet customers that we had so far only imagined.

How would we describe day one? After months of dreaming, more months of planning, and even more months than that of overcoming the frustrations of executing the plans, the first time you open your doors and face your customers is...exciting? Life changing? Thrilling? What would you guess?

Our answer is – terrifying! As you walk towards the door with the key in your hand for the first time, you realise – if you hadn't before – how much easier just dreaming about an idea is than actually making it happen.

We spent months immersed in a combination of enthusiasm and determination so we never had a moment to stop and question ourselves. We sailed towards opening with a wave of self-confidence and euphoria which stopped at precisely 7.00pm, the evening before we were to open our doors.

The night before opening was like the night before an important exam. Serious butterflies! All of a sudden the hubbub and activity of the past year was over and an eerie silence settled over our home. In the case of Coffee Republic, headquarters now was South Molton Street and not our living room, and suddenly all the paperwork and files that had been the centre of our lives for so long were there. We were hours from facing our public for the first time, and from seeing our dreams put to the test. We had controlled every variable we could have, and the others were beyond our control. Just like the night before an exam which we had studied and prepared for during a whole year, we were wondering what more we could do.

We can remember every strange and insignificant detail of that night, things like the light and the temperature and exactly what we did. All that bears testimony to how nervous we were. It was 3 November, when the clocks had just changed to winter daylight saving and one is not yet used to the early darkness. We put away our setting-up paperwork and our to-do list and found that there was one item remaining: To pick up the biscotti!

Biscotti being de rigeur in US espresso bar culture, Sahar was determined not to open without them. Although Italian biscotti were widely available in London, we felt it was an important part of our message to have the US style biscotti in the appropriate jars. These are much harder, so you can dip them into your drink to soften them and have very 'Coffee Republic' flavours like raspberry, vanilla and chocolate hazelnut.

Only at the last minute had Sahar learned about an American lady who baked them herself, and since they had a long cooking process (they have to be baked twice for some reason) she could only have them ready at 8.00 p.m. the night before opening.

So having picked up the biscotti we spent the night before our grand opening doing dress rehearsals with Tanya, Max and Miguel. The latter pair's English was slowly coming along as they got more and more confident with the Coffee Republic lingo of "e to flee", "skinny halfcaf decaf wet latte" that we had taught them!

The ever-loyal Eva was also there, making sure that our 5Ms were in order and doing everything she could to calm our unsteady nerves.

Nerves? We were nervous about everything you could worry about, especially the orders of supplies for the first day such as milk and food products. Ordering equipment had been easy because it was fixed and we had been able to visualise exactly how it would look. But supplies like milk and cakes weren't fixed. They depended on the customers and how many of these items they would order.

There was no way we could anticipate that or in any way control it. Should we order 20 blueberry muffins or 50 or 100? Should we order more carrot cake than chocolate cake? How many pints of milk? As much skimmed as whole? What about semi-skimmed? It was second-guessing what people would be ordering and unfortunately there was no textbook or magic formula to help us make the right guesses. If you have ever ordered at a restaurant for a friend you will understand how difficult this was.

In the end, we did things the most scientific way we could think of: we took a wild guess at all the orders and prayed that we would turn out not to be way off the mark! And so we arrived at:

Coffee Republic's opening day…
As you might imagine, neither of us slept very much that night! We were physically exhausted but mentally it was a 'toss and turn' night with the impending question echoing in both our heads: What if no one comes in? It wasn't a nightmare sort of worry so much as just a hidden and lingering doubt peeping out its head in darkness.

Sahar kept playing out the tune from Dirty Dancing, "please, please, please stay just a little bit longer…" visualising herself pleading with customers to spend more time sampling the delights of Coffee Republic.

So as you can well imagine, we were pacing the halls of our house at five in the morning, just hours from seeing our dream become a reality. We were relieved that it was not raining.

We had arbitrarily set opening time at 9.00am, figuring that the local shops opened at 10.00am, an hour later.

We had two deliveries that morning. Sahar went to pick up the croissants and pastries from St Quentin and Bobby went to Fulham Road to pick up the bagels. By 8.30am there was a small crowd gathered outside the shop. We couldn't believe it, but the people were shop assistants in the neighbouring stores whose curiosity had got the best of them.

Finally at 8.57am we ceremonially ripped off the brown paper and Max opened the door! Within minutes our 245 sq. ft. of space was over-crowded. A queue had already started. Real life: living, breathing customers! The rush took us by surprise as we had thought customers would come in gently, one-by-one and give us time to glide them through our wonderful menu. Instead, they came in droves as if we had been there forever and they had been having tall caramel lattes for years. Ridiculously, it occurred to us that the customers were making our beautiful shop look messy, and obscuring the view of all the food we had on display! By 11.00 am total chaos had ensued.

Tanya, Max and Miguel were rushed off their feet. We had run out of most of the food items and none of them had a minute to go to the basement for refills. Since the back counter area was small, there was nothing we could do on the other side. It was painful for us to see the empty displays and customers abandoning the long queue, but there was nothing we could do. It was as though the dialogue between Coffee Republic and its customers had already started and we were helpless to influence it in any way.

Thankfully a lot of our friends showed up to offer support and were incredibly helpful, especially when we asked them to stand outside as the store was overcrowded enough! When we ran out of skimmed milk one of them galloped over to Selfridge's food hall to buy us 15 pints.

They say that entrepreneurs should 'expect the unexpected'. Nothing rings more true. We had always visualised our perfect image of a Coffee Republic customer: screaming children was not it! For some reason or other we had never anticipated that those imaginary customers would come in with their kids. However, in reality it was a Christmas shopping Saturday and there were lots of children and frustrated, shopped-out exhausted ones at that; we could hardly say "its our first day, please kindly tell your children to not pour their juice all over our other customers!" Bobby got so frustrated over one errant child who had laid out her toys on our already crowded customer counters that a friend had to take him for a cooling walk round Hanover Square, hoping the child would not be there when they returned.

It could easily have been a comedy sketch. When Sahar, who normally considers receiving flowers to be one of the nicest gestures known to woman (or man!), received a bouquet of beautiful ones to congratulate her on the store opening, she was alarmed and panicked that they would overcrowd the already packed store. Not knowing what to do with them, she dumped them on a well wishing friend to somehow dispose of!

Thankfully Mr Lindop (the kind bank manager) who had threatened to visit didn't come. Amid the chaos and anarchy that was one extra thing we didn't need to deal with. And we both looked ashen enough already.

At the end of the longest day of our lives we closed the doors at 7.00 p.m. Tanya, Max and Miguel literally collapsed into a heap. We were lucky in that the next day was a Sunday and they could have a rest because otherwise they would have all walked out on us there and then. That day we made £500. It was amazing; we had expected £300 and our breakeven was £600. We felt like we had arrived.

In The Alchemist, Paulo Coelho describes a principle of 'favourability'. He says: "When you play cards the first time, you are almost sure to win. Beginner's luck...because there is a force that wants you to realize your destiny: it whets your appetite with a taste of success."

This aptly describes our first day. There was a lot of beginner's luck. It was basically the first Christmas shopping Saturday. Our share of beginner's luck ran out on the following Monday: we made only £215 – and it was the same for every weekday thereafter for months and months.

"Every search begins with beginner's luck. And every search ends with the victors being severely tested." - THE ALCHEMIST

January was a real shock for us. The euphoria of opening had passed, and our weekday sales were still in the low £200 range. We had even lost the Christmas shopping Saturdays.

To make matters worse, the inevitable teething problems that every new business experiences were beginning to surface. Bootstrapping is very much a short-term remedy and becomes impossible over an extended period of time, so this was no longer the answer to every challenge we faced.

Our personal delivery of croissants and bagels in the morning and sandwiches at lunchtime was becoming an exhausting drain on our time, not to mention being uneconomical. Since we had to park on a yellow line to deliver the goods, the cost of our parking fines far exceeded the turnover of sales.

The lady who was baking the muffins and fat-free cakes was not coping with the pressure of daily deliveries. She would turn up late some mornings and even asked once if she could not deliver at all the next day as she was planning a long weekend. Sahar had finally caught on to the fact that she had started delivering frozen muffins and just glazing them every morning to make them look freshly baked.

Our inexperience with employee issues was also surfacing. We cannot believe now that we used to do the barista weekly rotas ourselves. The shifts we allocated were probably too long. Working extended hours five days a week, Tanya, Max and Miguel were getting tired and unable to cope. We tried our best to re-motivate them but it was becoming an uphill struggle. We hired more employees (Max and Miguels' other friends from Pret) but since they weren't being managed properly, nothing helped.

Everything that could go wrong started to go wrong...
Employees would oversleep and open the store late. We used to get the milkman to leave the containers of milk outside the store in the early hours of the morning and half of them would be stolen by the time we arrived.

One day that we will never forget is when our espressos came out of the machine salty, and we mean very salty indeed. We filter the water we use for our coffee but what we had not been told by the supplier was that every month the filter had to be changed. If not, every espresso has the equivalent of three spoons of salt in it. That day, thank God, Sahar was the tenth customer. She still remembers the awful taste of her Latte and thinking that nine other customers were out there tasting a thoroughly disgusting liquid! Luckily they all came back. We gave each of them a free muffin as well as a replacement coffee and hoped that they would forgive us for our error.

Since that day Coffee Republic has a set rule that before opening each day, baristas have to taste the first three espressos themselves.

So on the one hand we were coping with the unexpected at each given moment, but on the other hand sales were remaining stagnant.

We remember so vividly sitting there at the window bench of the store every single day watching our target customers walk right past. The traffic was there, the office workers, the shoppers, the commuters we had talked about were all walking past our noses, but they were not coming in. They had their routines and it looked like we weren't a part of them. Even worse, a lot of them were walking past with polystyrene cups in hand but taking no interest in our store. They did not even have a mild curiosity about this totally new concept.

In order to get their attention every day after the morning rush we would send Max or Miguel outside onto the street offering samples. But even the sight of fully uniformed baristas offering free vanilla lattes and mini fat-free muffins was not working to break up these people's daily routine.

Where were all the girls who worked at Condé Nast? Sahar was convinced that skinny Lattes and fat-free muffins would lure them in but we never saw them. Sahar even set up a stall at London Fashion Week and personally gave out free lattes and brownies. Even that didn't make a difference.

Since there was little we could do until the sales started increasing, our daily chore of sitting in the store praying that people would come in was becoming increasingly demoralising. There we were, a lawyer and an investment banker in a 245 sq. ft. store, working day and night and not getting results. But somehow or other we just did not give up.

We did briefly consider doing that at the end of March, especially Bobby. But Sahar had left herself no choice but to make it work and she remained 100% committed in the deep belief that they were on to something great and sooner or later everyone else would tune in. Furthermore she had finally found the key to the treasure of loving your work and would never contemplate going back into the law.

Bobby, on the other hand, was in a totally different situation. He still had an open offer from Lehman Brothers. The stick holding the carrot was still dangling above his head and he still had a way out that was secure and very lucrative. He almost packed his bags in March when his ex-colleagues from Lehman were calling him in glee at their six figure bonuses and he had nothing to show for the work he'd been doing at Coffee Republic.

But Sahar's commitment and passion persuaded him to give it one more try. Sahar remembers the day matters came to a head vividly. It was the day after Easter Monday and she was doing the Coffee Republic bills on the kitchen table when Bobby broke the news that he was considering giving up.

There was no way she could think of that she could persuade Bobby to change his mind as she knew the weakness in her argument was that she was very emotional about Coffee Republic. Although every business needs someone with passion and emotion, business decisions need to be made entirely dispassionately. Sahar knew that she felt too passionately about Coffee Republic to be able to offer a rational business argument for Bobby to stay.

So she phoned a mutual friend, George, who was extremely intelligent and always put things clearly and didn't mince his words. Bobby respected his judgement, but Sahar's secret weapon was that she knew George had always thought that Coffe Republic was a fabulous idea.

George entered the picture and within a day of back and forth bantering with Bobby he persuaded Bobby to stay. We will both never forget what he did for us that day which proves that there is a lot to be said for having support from friends at moments when your spirit is waning.

It's often said that it's always darkest just before dawn, but that dawn never fails to arrive. This may be true, but whatever we went through during those first six months, we can tell you it was dark indeed. Sometimes we seriously wondered when, or even if, the daylight would start shining through.

Napoleon Hill, in his classic bestseller, Think and Grow Rich, refers to the PERSISTENCE TEST. He believes that "there is a hidden guide whose duty is to test people through all sorts of discouraging experiences. Those who pick themselves up after defeat and keep on trying, arrive and then the world cries 'Bravo! I knew you could do it!' The hidden guide lets no one enjoy great achievement without passing the PERSISTENCE TEST."

For Coffee Republic, dawn broke in the first week of April.

Having been entirely ignored by the press up to that point, we finally got our first article in, believe it or not, Aer Lingus' inflight magazine. No fewer than 60 people turned up brandishing a copy of the issue in which it appeared. At the same time Tyler Brule, the founder of the visionary *Wallpaper magazine, was at the

Independent on Sunday and wrote an influential article about the new buzzword 'third place' and pronounced Coffee Republic as an example of a new 'affordable luxury.'

Articles followed in Vogue and Tatler's April issues. Vogue said "For anyone who thought coffee choice stopped at black or white, Coffee Republic's selection is awesome". They recommended our Cinnamon Lattes and as a result, sales of Cinnamon Lattes soared.

The articles had an immediate impact on our sales. The curve was finally tipping upwards, in our favour.

WE HAD PASSED THE PERSISTENCE TEST!

With the new surge of energy we had gained from the press interest we still worked to tweak the concept further. We wanted to get a broad customer base and were realizing that we were attracting mainly upmarket customers. The press articles highlighted this by referring to our 'Eva Jiricna designed haven'. This is when we knew we had made a mistake by making the bar look too highly designed and stark and therefore a bit intimidating to the average man on the Clapham omnibus (a phrase Sahar picked up during her legal days).

Since it was out of question to spend any money on any sort of redesign we had one of those 'gut-instinct entrepreneurial moments' and thought that perhaps our stark white walls were the problem. So one Sunday we went to Homebase on the Warwick Road and bought two cans of the most untrendy caramel beige paint that we could find on the colour chart. It was the sort that would have horrified Eva Jiricna or anyone with the remotest semblance of taste!

There was a bit of a sibling scuffle in the middle of Homebase as Sahar was equally horrified by the colour and protested vehemently (yes, tears were shed) that we were at risk of losing any of the 'cool' kudos we had so laboriously earned! But Bobby proved right. The colour change to something warmer worked; the caramel beige tone immediately made the store much more friendly.

A week later we saw what we had envisaged all along – the man driving the rubbish bin truck down South Molton street stopped outside our store and queued up for his Grande Mocha along with businessmen, shop assistants and fashionistas. For us, this moment was a real feeling of achievement. We had read somewhere that "not everyone can afford a luxury car, luxury holiday or a luxury meal but everyone can afford a luxury coffee". And we had succeeded in providing it.

The wonderful thing about having a great product is that you only need to get people to try it once. We 'converted' customers one at a time by giving them a positive experience. Word of mouth took care of the rest.

We did not use any traditional 'marketing tactics' because we didn't really know any. We just knew that the only way each customer would come back day after day was if we delivered a consistently high quality experience each time. That experience would become the 'luxury' part of the customer's everyday routine. We knew this, because we knew that would be what would make us come back as customers if we ourselves were in their shoes – and we were already in their shoes, so it all worked out!

Mixed in with all the hard work, fears and worries there were some humorous moments too. Our funniest story happened when, after much persuading, we gained permission from the council to put two benches outside the South Molton Street store. This was an idea which Sahar had picked up in a Spring Street coffee bar in New York's SoHo and had always dreamt of doing for Coffee Republic. The thinking was that benches allow you to sit out and watch the world go by while sipping your iced Latte.

We had found from the yellow pages THE company that supplied park benches and after much study we ordered two 'Mendips' (you will be surprised to learn that park benches come in about twenty shapes and sizes, but 'Mendip' was our style with thick handles to allow resting of the coffee cup).

We were anxious for delivery of the Mendips by April as spring weather was making London a glorious place to sit and sip. As you can probably guess, delivery of popular items always takes longer than one hopes or expects.

On the proposed date of delivery, Sahar was sitting at home waiting for a call from the South Molton Street manager to confirm arrival of the benches. By midday no call had come through and Sahar was getting impatient. Funnily enough, just as she was thinking of chasing up the factory, she was distracted by what appeared to be a terrible traffic jam along the idyllically quiet and leafy Kensington street. There were cars hooting and a murmur of drivers getting out of their cars to direct traffic. She realised to her horror that an articulated lorry about 40 feet long was trying to turn into their tiny residential road. As the said vehicle, trailing the destruction of neighbourhood peace in its wake, turned into their road Sahar saw to her great embarrassment the picture of Mendip-like benches painted on its side. They were delivering the Mendips to the house!

After redirecting the driver, South Molton Street acquired its benches and the Mendips, just like the Pied Piper, drew in locals who would almost sit on top of each other enjoying the threesome of great coffee, front row seats at the daily South Molton Street parade of London's trendiest, and the joys of the city in the spring.

The story doesn't end there, though. One morning a week later, Sahar was rushing to secure prime seating on the Mendip before the shopkeepers arrived to discover that the benches were gone, leaving a gaping void where they had once stood!

In the middle of the night they had been stolen. A lorry must have drawn up and swept them away. It still amazes us to ponder who would buy second-hand park benches, and stolen ones at that. This taught us the big lesson: to chain the replacement set to the shop-front for safekeeping. When later we detected an attempt to cut the chains our poor baristas had to take the benches in every night – not an easy task!

The lessons we learnt from our first six months of actually being a business were:

Law 47: Don't expect customers to flock in. Success is not an entitlement

They, like the rest of the world, don't accept new ideas easily. Good things take time.

Coffee Republic was not an instant success, as you now know from reading our story. Although we were lucky in that we caught on to the coffee boom at the right time, even then nothing fell into our laps. We had to work for everything.

You have to assume that customers, just like every other hurdle you pass (bankers, suppliers, agents etc.,) will not buy into your vision initially.

Law 48: It won't be easy at the beginning. You need stickability

It's your duty as the entrepreneur to keep on believing and pass the persistence test. Never give up!

The difference between entrepreneurs you hear about and those you don't is only that the ones you hear about never gave up. There are so many obstacles along the path of the entrepreneurial journey that you need 'stickability'. Even when you have your business up and running you still need to draw on the bank of commitment that got you there in the first place.

Law 49: Keep focused

The extraordinary paradox of entrepreneurship is how much you are constantly swimming against the tide and how much you have to stick to your guns no matter how far along you are in the journey. What happened to us was that after all the hard work we had done to open, our sales were very slow at the beginning.

At that point all the pressure starts to build and the pessimists and doomsayers start to say "I told you so".

What we did instead was to stick to our guns and not give in to the pressure to change our focus. We kept focusing on the coffee experience and believing in the added value we were offering. It took six months but it finally paid off. If you believed in the first place that your idea was a good one, and all your research supports that conclusion, then why give up at the first sign of trouble? Don't become an entrepreneur, though, if you're expecting to walk in to an easy life.

Law 50: It's a marathon not a sprint! Look after yourself

Since at the start-up stage you are so closely connected with the identity of the business it is imperative that you take care of YOURSELF. Leave time for exercise, relaxation and pampering. Eat healthily and occasionally indulge yourself in the little luxuries of life, in whatever makes a positive difference to your well-being. If you let yourself go, your business will slowly be affected. Sacrificing your own well being for your business will in the long term affect the business itself. The business is an extension of you.

Conventional theory suggests that founders should look dishevelled, unkempt and exhausted – it's a sign of hard work. It's not! It's a sign that you're not managing your time properly. You need energy, stamina and strong self-belief for the long, arduous road ahead. An investor once told us that he starts to get worried once he sees founders he has invested in beginning to lose control of their physical appearance. For him it's the first sign of trouble.

So keep taking care of yourself. The stronger and happier you are, the stronger and happier your business will be.

It's not over 'till the fat lady sings". Nothing is more true for the entrepreneurial journey. You are constantly being tested and you have to constantly persist. A lot of entrepreneurs say of their journey that it's always more difficult than you anticipate and takes longer than you expect, but that is itself the beauty of the journey. It is like climbing Everest, the thrill keeps you on such a high that you sail through obstacles without realising that they are there.

And that's where we found ourselves in April 1996. The obstacles and the doubts and fears were a distant memory. We had reached breakeven and every day our sales, the loyalty to our concept and our brand recognition was climbing on an upward curve. The tide had finally turned in our favour.

Remember a 1% difference everyday makes a 100% difference in just over three months!

CHAPTER EIGHT:
GROWING
FROM BIRTH TO MATURITY

To grow or not to grow?

Your business is up and running. Technically, at this stage you have 'done it'. You have fulfilled every goal set out in your business plan. You have implemented your dream 100%.

So, is time to put up your feet for a well-earned rest? Or perhaps to break out the champagne and sit back while business takes care of itself, now that all the hard work is done? If that's what you're thinking, you should be so lucky! If you sit back now, your business is likely to disappear before you're finished with the celebratory meal.

Now you have to move to the next stage of business life.

Law 51: There is no plateau - you either go up or down

Here's a cold hard reality for you to ponder: at any given time, your business can only be going one of two ways. Up. Or down. There is no such thing as a plateau. In business, such a thing just doesn't exist. Statistics show that a business cannot stagnate and stay small, nor can it ever entertain the notion of hoping to be nothing more than stable. A business either evolves, or it dies.

The reason for this is that a business is a living thing, like a human being.

It follows the same pattern of growth of a human being by passing through several successive stages. Just as child cannot become an adult without going through youth, in a similar way businesses have to pass through defined stages of growth. These stages are smooth, though they do involve complex transitional periods.

"There is actually a formal school of theory called the 'life-cycle model of business growth' based on a biological analogy of the maturing of human beings which underlines this point. The lifecycle model states that " just as humans pass through similar stages of physiological and psychological development – so do businesses evolve in predictable ways and encounter similar problems in their growth. Managers of firms at different stages of growth have different tasks and priorities just as parents of children of different ages face different challenges."

- AMAR BHIDE, The Origin and Evolution of New Businesses

As your business evolves and changes naturally, you will be vulnerable to failure if you don't anticipate the next stage because everything around you changes as well. The market will change, the operating environment will change, and you will find few of the things you deal with are constant. You will not be able to cope with the increasing pressure from competitors nor with the pressures increased sales will put on your business unless you have thought about them before they happen.

So whatever you decide to do, whether it's:

☐ grow,

☐ stay small,

☐ or throw in the towel,

you have to appreciate that you can't stagnate because your business is evolving and you have to think about the next stage and make an informed decision about it.

Before you make any decision, consider whether you are ready for growth.

PREPARATION FOR GROWTH

Are you ready?

If you want your business to grow then you face a harsh lesson in reality. Going back to the analogy we used earlier, when children grow their personality changes and the same will be true of your business. Growth means adding new people to your team, and new structures and layers to your company. It's a big time commitment, and it means that you have to be ready to up the ante. It also means that you will be letting go, to some extent, of the child you originally brought into the world. Your business is, in some ways, about to leave its small, familiar face behind (which was closely aligned with that of its founder) and take new steps towards a life of its own. Entrepreneurs often have difficulty coming to terms with this reality.

Is the business ready?

Have you anticipated and planned for changes in your business as it gets bigger? Is your business ready to hire and manage more people? Are the controls and systems in place? If you've just launched a business, such issues probably seem a million miles away but, nevertheless, you cannot start mulling them over in your mind early enough.

Is the market ready?

Is the market big enough to sustain your growth? This is a key question you'll face almost as soon as you're established. Is there enough demand out there? Are the customers there? How is the competition reacting to your arrival, and what plans for the future do they have? Have you established market presence? Is the future of the market looking good? Are the trends in your favour? All of these factors are essentially external to your own organisation and lie largely outside your control. Nevertheless, you need to be monitoring the answers to the questions above on a daily basis so that you will know when the time is right to make the move to develop your business. And, if you have been planning ahead, your business will be primed for growth when the right market conditions do arrive.

Is your company financially ready?
Money is a key component of growth. If your organisation is ready to grow and the market opportunity is there, you will inevitably still need cash to capitalise on the potential that lies ahead.

Do you have enough cash to grow or do you need to raise money for growth? Are your accounting systems strong enough? Do you know how much cash you need and when? Are the numbers looking good enough to attract outside investors?

Law 52: A warning - monitor your speed. Growth can kill

You have to be ready for growth from a personal perspective as well as from the point of view of the market, your business and your bank account. It's an enormous mistake to grow before you are ready. In fact, that sort of premature growth will kill your business.

Just as you cannot be born at five years old, you can't suddenly turn your business into an empire overnight. Growth has to go through its stages, just like the growth of a human being. You cannot become an adult without going through the chaotic changes of adolescence. You cannot become a child unless you are nurtured as a baby.

We have seen good retail concepts try to become chains too quickly and thus not allowing their business plans to evolve organically through the required stages. These businesses are not nurtured, and as a result they do not grow up properly. When stages are skipped, pressure is put on other points in theevolutionary cycle and as result, eventually everything implodes. First, the quality of product or service declines and the downfall snowballs from there. If you want an example, look at the recent Internet boom. Some people have argued that dot.coms demonstrated that thinking on growth potential had changed and that it was possible to emerge from the womb fully formed without having to pass through the early stages that are usually inevitable for a business. But look what has now happened as a result. The dot.com crash underlines that in business growth terms, there are no shortcuts.

So if you choose growth, be aware that you have to have the same patience, persistence and commitment you had at the beginning. You cannot take a growth pill. It's not something you graduate towards. It's a long process.

If you have decided that you are not ready for growth, or you don't aspire to having a big business (with headaches and glory attached) then **STOP HERE.**

But be warned of the dangers of staying small. You could be putting a finite end to your success. Know that somewhere along the line some new brash kid's going to come on the block and steal your thunder. You did it to start; someone will do it to you. So keep your ear firmly to the ground.

Whatever you decide, we've got a good growth story to tell you.

Our Story: A tale of change

We never sat back and actually thought about growth. It was always inevitable for us that it would be part of the plan. The exact words in that first business plan were "Coffee Republic is committed to establishing itself not just as another coffee shop, but as a leading brand of espresso bar concept in the UK."

The 'chain' bit was part of our light bulb. Our original idea was a to have a Coffee Republic on every high-pedestrian count street corner. So growth was part and parcel of our entrepreneurial attitude.

We could probably write a whole book just about our growth from 1 to 100 stores in five years. This was a rate of store opening that saw Coffee Republic named the second fastest growing company in the UK in 2002 by Deloite Touche. However, we won't attempt to give you the full story. If we did this book would have to be about management and business. This book is not about that, nor is it about Coffee Republic the company. It's the story of the entrepreneurial journey of its founders. And by definition as a company grows it becomes more a story about management and business rather than about entrepreneurship. So in this section we will relate the personal tale of the entrepreneurs through the hyper-growth of the company.

That tale is one of change. The entrepreneur in the early days of the business has to act like a force of nature, breathing life into an idea through a combination of creativity and energy, discipline and organisation. Certain qualities, as we have pointed out, are needed to succeed. The qualities needed to manage and grow an established business are not the same. In fact they are as different as you can imagine. The successful business is less reliant on inspiration and more reliant on a system of checks and balances. Suddenly, the business given life by your personality needs you to become all the things that would have hindered success at the outset. Now, to help the company you founded you need to take on the attributes of a regular, every day employee – and that, for a founder, is not easy.

To simplify things as we tell the story, we have decided to label the growth phases of Coffee Republic in a way similar to the development of a human being. You will see what we faced as we move through each phase; through each one there was a slow evolution to the next level.

THE BABY YEARS – we refer to are those when Coffee Republic had one to six stores. This is the period when the founders and the business itself were indistinguishable from each other: like a baby, the business was totally helpless and needed us to take care of its every last consideration.

THE CHILDHOOD YEARS – were between 7 stores and 25, a period when Coffee Republic was starting to take on a life of its own. It started to walk and talk independently, to acquire a personality of its own. Others started to take an interest in it. Yet it still needed the help and guidance of the entrepreneurs. At this time, there was a move from the kitchen table to the first office.

THE ADOLESCENT YEARS – happened as the business grew up and matured. The turbulent adolescent period involved a change in the balance between the empire of the entrepreneur and the onset of an independent organisational culture, which has taken root as the organisation has grown larger. Think growing pains and rebellion!

THE ADULT YEARS – were above the 80 stores level, when we realised as entrepreneurs that our creation had turned into a fully responsible, mature adult with its own identity. The business was no longer entrepreneurial in nature and therefore put into question our own individual roles.

THE BABY YEARS

It's April 1996...one store is up and running.

The thing about the growth of retail chains is that growth equals cloning. Once you have the concept right you take the DNA and, in effect, clone it. The bigger the chain the more clones you have. However, if there is anything wrong with the first concept – the DNA – then any new stores will just multiply the problems as you produce defective clones. Our first task was thus getting the DNA of South Molton Street right.

In order to do this, the most important role for an entrepreneur at the beginning – when the business first becomes operational – is to stay very close to everything; keep close to customers and to every single detail.

By keeping a close eye you will need to do two things with the new business:

Law 53: You will need to adapt and tweak your original concept

The reason it's imperative that you do this is because while you were dreaming and planning your business you were basing it all on your gut instinct and a lot of ballpark numbers, guesswork and assumptions. This changes once your doors are open. Whereas before your ideas were untested and unvalidated, you now have real customers and you can really see what works and what doesn't. The only way you can get a detailed picture of reality is by involving yourself day-to-day in everything that happens.

By seeing for yourself unforeseen problems and even opportunities, you will be able to adapt and modify your original idea. However, be warned that there is a fine line between modifying your offer to suit customer needs and changing your focus.

As we told you in our story, there will always be a lot of pressure to change focus because the inclination of the universe at the beginning is to tell you that your idea won't work (it's the credibility issue again). You have to be involved because it is not enough to rely on a store manager or someone else to tell you what does and doesn't sell, etc. If you keep a close eye on the details with your big vision in mind you will be sensitive to any adaptations that are needed, and you will be able to make them without giving up on your idea.

We already told you how we adapted our concept to make it more approachable (for example, the caramel beige paint from Homebase). We also focused more on the health theme and 'skinny' (skimmed milk) angle which was then catching on.

Law 54: Bootstrapping is not a long term strategy. Time to upgrade your resources

It's a fact of entrepreneurship that as a start-up you will not attract the resource providers that you need, so you make do with what you have and bootstrap. But you can't do that for long. It's not a long-term remedy. We learned through the nightmares of the teething problems that we have already told you about (the parking tickets for our croissant delivery, the supplier asking to take the weekend off) that we had underestimated the importance of two things: choosing suppliers and hiring people. However great the product, the look, the brand, and all the other details, what really mattered was delivering consistency to the customer day after day, 7.00 a.m. to 7.00 p.m. We learned that one bad experience undoes one hundred great ones.

Upgrading suppliers.
We really learnt a lesson in South Molton Street about how difficult life can be for a retail business if suppliers are unprofessional and inconsistent. We knew we would have to make changes in our suppliers if we were to contemplate more than one store or even be able to maintain that one store. With greater numbers, we wouldn't possibly be able to clock-watch supplier arrival times every morning as we were doing at the start!

With suppliers being one of the most crucial components of an expanding business, we set out to upgrade to more established and professional companies who could deliver quality and handle delivering large volumes to multiple sites nationally.

By this time the bigger suppliers were becoming aware of the potential of espresso bars. They could no longer ignore them or deem the idea to be crazy, and as such businesses were up and running suppliers were realising that they were missing out if they did not get in on the act themselves. By the time we contacted them all again they had more time for us and were willing to change their recipes to accommodate our needs.

The boom was also bringing new suppliers to the market, specifically aimed at meeting the needs of the US-style coffee bars. Within a year of our opening, all sorts of suppliers that hadn't existed before had opened their doors, including a specialist muffin supplier (who already had fat-free muffins among its products!) which we would have given the world for six months earlier.

We can't believe now that we used to order our coffee-making accessories such as foaming milk thermometers and shot glasses from a catalogue company in the US and have them shipped over by FedEx before each store opening. Within a couple of months even an espresso accessory company had sprouted up. A UK company even started manufacturing our special take-away cups.

The moral here, particularly if your business is an innovative one, is to keep looking for help. The more you prove your credibility, the more likely you are to be surprised to find that the market will move to meet your needs and you will be able to source things that, at first, did not exist. The success of your business can give a boost to help other businesses launch or expand in its wake.

Strengthening the Team
We soon learned that however much we controlled the variables, ultimately the Coffee Republic customer experience really took place directly between the customer and our baristas. The quality of the customer experience depended ultimately on the quality

of employees: how they greeted them, how quickly they served them and the quality of the drink prepared. Especially because our concept of tailor made drinks was new, employees acted as important marketers, in position to educate customers and recommend new drinks.

With our employees playing such a critical role in developing our brand identity and building a loyal customer base we knew that we had to focus on hiring and training well-qualified and highly motivated individuals. The problem was that such people are not attracted to start-ups with little in the way of track record. Most people look instead for job security and a future, neither of which a start-up can guarantee.

As we told you in the last chapter, our lack of operational skills and experience was coming to the surface as our sales increased and put increased demands on employee hours. We didn't know how to manage our staff and we couldn't attract good managers to manage them either!

We had found a good source of hourly employees through the BUNAC scheme, which provides a pool of US students looking for part-time work in the UK. The advantage for us was that most of them were familiar with our concept, having been used to it in the US.

But what was the point of having a good pool of employees if we couldn't manage them? We think that the last straw for us was in the summer of 1996 when we were taking an investor (who became our angel investor) to South Molton Street for the first time, having told him all day about our strict coffee focus. Upon entering the bar we found one of the baristas was making a salad for herself on the back counter! It was such a let down for us!

Looking back, that summer we had so many near disasters. It was just our luck that the summer months amounted to one long heat wave and we could not afford to put air-conditioning in the store. Employees were almost getting heat stroke at work, especially as we wanted them to keep their baseball caps on and these were made of pure wool. On one particularly hot day that we will never forget, the fridge and the till broke down at the same time and the milk was curdling. We were beside ourselves with panic!

However, the good news was that as we were getting more press coverage and the coffee craze was taking root in the public's mind, we were slowly attracting a better and better quality of employee. We were finally saved from a string of catastrophic hires by a new Operations Manager. He was the perfect fit for the first key professional member of our new team. Although he had solid experience in fast food brands he wasn't the 'big business' type so he fitted in very nicely into our entrepreneurial team.

It was such a relief. The responsibility of hiring and managing employees was no longer down to the two of us. That was a hat we could now delegate to a specialist. One thing off our list!

So by staying close to the business we had adapted the concept, upgraded our suppliers and employees, and set the foundation for growth. The DNA of the original clone was set right. What about the market, was it ready?

Preparing for growth: the market
In April 1996, our market was heating up. In fact, the state of the coffee market was making our growth imperative. The coffee boom was frothing in the UK and the BBC was proclaiming the arrival of 'a coffee revolution'. A great race for market share was taking shape and our main competitor, the Seattle Coffee Company, had already opened three stores.

In other words, everything was moving quickly. Coffee bars were sprouting up all over the place. Some of them were genuine attempts at US style concepts whilst others just involved bandwagon jumpers looking for a new craze. They say that it only took one person to break the four-minute mile record and that once he did it, everyone was able to follow. We think this is what was happening in the coffee market. Everyone who had harboured the seed of the coffee idea was encouraged by the likes of Coffee Republic and Seattle to actually give it a try. Even sandwich bars and restaurants were dressing up their coffee offer.

It was as though the whole world was sticking coffee beans in their windows; we were hot. The UK had woken up and it was smelling the coffee.

As a first mover in the market, we needed to move fast and capitalise on the goodwill and recognition we had built. So many customers were coming up to us and saying "I wish you could open a Coffee Republic near my home, my sister's, my offices…" So with us ready, the business ready, the DNA complete and the market ready the only thing we didn't have was money.

Preparing for growth: the finance

As we had done for our first store, we sat back at our desks to write a new business plan to address our next stage and to raise money for it. This time we were looking to open not one store but another six.

This time we could write a 'real' business plan. We knew the business and our concept was now tried and tested. The numbers were real. In the first business plan all our figures had been ballpark guesses in a business which we knew nothing about. But after the first store we no longer needed to use estimates. We had real numbers to work with. It was a joy to deal with the tangible!

For the first nine months we had done all the company's accounting ourselves. The manager would call us with final till sales every night, leaving them on our home answerphone. We remember it used to determine our mood for the rest of the evening. We would take the till receipts home at night and analyse sales, pay suppliers, write employee paycheques and balance it all in a cash book. Although this was quite cumbersome it was important for us to stay close to the finances in order to really understand the business in detail and get the financial DNA right for the rollout.

Like bootstrapping this was the only way for us to find out what the real opening and operating costs were, how quickly we could reach breakeven, and what margins we could actually expect to achieve. Bobby put together a financial model for the rollout based on the actual performance of our first store. Our model depended on sales reaching breakeven so once our weekly sales for South

Molton Street reached that point, we knew we had a good financial model for growth.

We now had a clear understanding of how much money we needed to open each outlet. Our rollout plan was for 25 stores in three years, but we wanted to start the first phase by opening six new stores in a year. To achieve this goal, we needed to raise £600,000.

We knew that for this amount, loans were not really an option. So we had to accept the fact that in order to raise the money we needed, we would have to give away shares in our company. For the first time, we would have to give away a piece of our business.

We were reluctant to go to mainstream venture capital funds, as we were worried that they would require too big a chunk of the business in return for their investment. While we were considering what to do as an alternative, Bobby came across an advert in the Financial Times for the Venture Capital Report (VCR). He had never heard of VCR but the advert offered everything he had been looking for.

"VCR is UK's longest running agency for linking investors and entrepreneurial businesses seeking equity capital. VCR is published monthly and features the business proposals of entrepreneurs seeking capital between £2000 and £2m. VCR's 750 subscribers are predominantly private investors popularly referred to as 'business angels'." We immediately placed an advert in the May issue.

Coffee Republic

£600,000

Coffee Republic, a novel coffee bar concept based on successful US models, was founded by Bobby and Sahar Hashemi. The first outlet, in South Molton Street, was opened on 4 November 1996, with the aid of DTI backed funding, and has now passed breakeven level with sales exceeding £700 per day in the week ending 20 April. Each new outlet will cost an average of £85,000 to open, and it is planned to expand to 25 outlets within three years. £600,000 is sought to finance the first phase of expansion. 40% of the equity is offered.

The Concept and the Pilot

Bobby and Sahar Hashemi, a brother and sister team, founded Coffee Republic to replicate, in the UK, a concept which has been immensely successful in the US. A number of highly profitable chains of specialised coffee bars have been established in the US in the past three years, including Starbucks. Starbucks, the market leader, has grown from 17 espresso bars in 1987 to over 800 today. Believing that the concept could be successfully transposed to the UK, the Hashemis put together a business plan for Coffee Republic, their own vision of the concept that would flourish in the UK. They obtained the backing of the DTI with a Small Firms Loan Guarantee Scheme of £78,000. Their aim is "*to introduce a new coffee experience, superior to anything present in the UK market today...based on serving a creative selection of espresso-based beverages at affordable prices in convenient locations.*"

The pilot outlet for Coffee Republic opened in South Molton Street, London, on 4 November 1995. The weekly sales figures that have been achieved to date are shown in Table A. Sales have been steadily increasing to the current level of c £4,400 per week, exceeding the breakeven level for the outlet. Mr Hashemi is confident that sales will continue to increase substantially. The outlet has received wide press coverage in articles covering the new coffee boom in the UK, including *The Independent on Sunday, The Observer, Vogue, Tatler,* and *Caterer & Hotelkeeper.*

The outlet itself comprises 275 sq ft of retail space, with floor to ceiling

Bobby Hashemi standing outside Coffee Republic

Coffee Republic's South Molton Street Outlet

Law 55: Go with smart money.
Angels bring in experience as well as money

Phone calls started pouring in the day the issue came out. 'Business Angels' were exactly what we needed at this stage, especially as most of them were successful business people and thus brought with them the added advantage of their own business expertise. We were so thrilled to get calls of interest from well-known business figures that wanted to invest in us. A lot of them had seen the booming coffee concept in the US first hand and they were very interested in buying into the process of bringing it to the UK.

We were inundated with offers as we started meeting potential investors. It felt like they were interviewing us but we were also interviewing them. Bringing in an outside investor is like bringing someone into your home. It's more than the money; you need to get along and have same vision and outlook.

Law 56: Don't just accept the first cheque you are offered
– Bringing in an investor is like inviting someone to live
in your home

We interviewed all of our prospective angels on the sofa in our living room. We chatted together a lot to make sure we agreed on the important things. It became obvious to us quickly which people we couldn't work with or, more often, we wouldn't want to work with. Some were too pushy and intrusive and even in the interviews were already telling us what to do!

We finally met the right match, though it wasn't obvious to us from the start. We had met lots of angels who looked exactly like you imagine a serious, high-net-worth angel should look like, but this one was totally out of the ordinary. Hip, trendy and eccentric are words he wouldn't mind us using to describe him. As with the first bank manager's appearance, we were deceived once again. He was a hugely successful entrepreneur, had founded a very well-known brand which he had sold and this was just his style. We got on well with him instantly.

He trusted us as people and trusted the vision we had for the concept. We spent quite a bit of time with him sharing our vision. We took him around the competition. He was the one we were with in South Molton Street when, after explaining to him that we were 'entirely coffee focused', we noticed one of our baristas making herself a salad on the back counter!

In turn, we instantly trusted him and valued his experience and expertise. Most importantly, we enjoyed sharing our dreams with him. In fact our choice was one of the best decisions we ever made and he is to this day a big part of Coffee Republic. Incidentally he exited having made five times his original investment.

Law 57: Don't get too many small investors on board

The only condition he had was that he wanted to be the only investor and as such he was willing to put up the entire sum we needed. This worked perfectly for us, as there is nothing worse than having many small investors you need to report to, which can take up an enormous amount of time. This is distracting for you and for the business. We quickly signed all the paperwork and by July were ready to embark on our next stage of growth.

Preparing for growth: the business

Our angel money arrived in the bank in July and immediately we embarked on the next stage of our growth. Basically, we received the £600,000 we needed in two tranches. The big relief was that we were for the first time able to draw ourselves a salary. At £30,000 each it was still much less than anything we could have been earning if we had stuck to our old jobs, but it was better than nothing at all.

Another great thing was that our angel introduced us to someone who was to play a big part in the growth of Coffee Republic. Our paperwork and accounting, already cumbersome, was going to be unmanageable for us to do with more than one store. So our angel brought our first accountant, Marco Donghi, into our life.

Every Friday he would come over and on our kitchen table we would hand over all the till receipts and paperwork, and pay all the bills and pay cheques. He had a day job so he did Coffee Republic work in the evening for the first nine months.

The arrival of the money also meant that, for the first time, we were in a position to strenghten our branding and marketing message. We could afford to hire a designer to do a proper logo. This was a key item remaining on our list of things to do before opening the second store. We wanted our graphics and image to finally be absolutely right. For the first opening we had very much bootstrapped and done all our graphics (mostly ourselves) on a tight budget. Now with the concept successful and money in the bank we could afford to spend time fine-tuning in the quest for making our message laser sharp.

We knew that our logo wasn't strong and distinctive enough to establish brand presence across London. It was easily copyable and had already been imitated by a coffee bar on Gloucester Road.

We still did not want to go to the big brand agencies, firstly because we couldn't afford them even with the new funds and secondly because we had a good idea of what we wanted and didn't need the skills of a big agency to inspire us. Through a bit of investigation we found an agency that was a perfect fit for us called Formation. It was they who had designed the graphics and packaging for Pret A Manger. We loved what they had done for the food and sandwiches packaging at Pret. They had managed to capture and project the soul of the brand, and we wanted them to do the same with coffee for us.

As an agency they were also close to us in spirit. They were a small entrepreneurial company started by Adrian Kilby who, though he had surrounded himself with a great team, was still involved himself in every aspect of his business. Through his years with the Pret founders Adrian was fairly accustomed to the whims and demands of passionate entrepreneurs.

Since we were spending our entire marketing budget on graphics, we decided not to hire architects and to design store interiors ourselves with the help of Formation.

In the summer of 1996 we spent day after day with Adrian and his team at their studios in Clerkenwell coming up with the graphics package we wanted. There was a lot of soul searching, pouring over New York photos, looking at competitors, until finally we came up with what we think of as our first proper identity.

We had a lot of sibling arguments about graphics. The great thing about being siblings is that there are no politics: you say whatever you believe and you fight your corner without incurring the wrath of the other.

Coffee Republic has benefited from our honesty with each other and, thank God, Adrian and his team took our bickering with much patience and consideration. Adrian once suggested he buy us foam hammers so we could hit each other whenever (and it was often) we disagreed!

We call the branding exercise we went through with Adrian and his team our 'Statue of Liberty' phase. What we wanted to do was reinforce our concept's New York origins, both to differentiate ourselves from the Seattle Coffee Company and to suggest a flattering affinity between cosmopolitan London and the Big Apple. (Later on, once we had established the brand, we dropped the New York theme.)

Looking back at the graphics we developed with the perspective of hindsight, we can see what a genuine reflection they were of the soul of Coffee Republic.

Growing...
With the new logo designed, an experienced operations manager in position, new suppliers set, and funds in the bank we really felt ready to find the second store.

The great thing about the passage of time and growth is that all the rules we told you earlier about credibility and suppliers and resources not being there start tipping in your favour. Our credibility was far more established and the site-finding process was now definitely easier as property agents knew that we were serious and landlords could see photos of our concept. As a result, we spent far less time finding a second site than we had had to spend on the first.

The site we settled on was on Great Marlborough Street (just off Carnaby Street) and the second Coffee Republic store opened in December 1996. It was geographically close to South Molton Street and it had the same profile of customers. It was also convenient moving baristas and materials as required between the two stores as they were only a five-minute walk apart. Since we were monitoring both stores closely, this was another plus for us – it would have been much more difficult if the second store had been on the other side of London.

The advent of the second store changed little about the business in real terms, but for us the big thrill was that we had evolved into a chain, albeit a small one for the time being. We remained very hands on in the running of the business, and simply had double the work!

Even though our evolution was well underway (we had technically doubled in size), we still refer to these days as the baby years because the business and ourselves were still one and we nurtured its every move. Although resources were starting to tip in our favour it was only a little move; we still had to bootstrap and make two plus two equal five.

To give you an example, in those days chocolate covered espresso beans were all the rage and we decided that, being coffee focused, we had to have them in our stores. However, since the amounts we were ordering were too small for the factory to package we decided to buy them in bulk and package them ourselves. Boxes of bulk espresso beans arrived in a container at our flat in three flavours. We found suppliers of clear bags, ribbons and logoed stickers and, using our mini kitchen scales we packaged the espresso beans at home.

In fact, the night before opening our second store, it took us until early morning to finish the job, which had quite a calming effect.

It just goes to prove that entrepreneurs also spend time working on an assembly line: thank heaven we had two friends from New York staying who helped us finish the job. We had specified 125g. per pack and by end of the night we were so tired we could hardly get the grams right. Every time it went over we would eat the outstanding balance. A thoroughly unprofessional approach, but it got the job done!

Our espresso beans almost sold out on the first day so the next night we had to make another batch, and by Christmas our flat was looking more like a stock room and distribution centre for candy than a home.

In February 1997 we opened our third store on Queensway. This was situated on a corner and had previously been an ice cream parlour. It was quite oddly shaped with only a very small entrance but we were desperate for a third store to catch up with Seattle Coffee Company so we went with the location.

The redeeming feature of Queensway was that the store had a basement which we turned into Coffee Republic's first proper offices. We moved the Ops Manager there and finally having an office enabled us to hire Marco, who had been working on our accounting at nights, full time. We remember the excitement of actually having an office, but unfortunately there was no room for us, so we carried on working from home.

We also converted part of the basement into something we had always dreamed of: The Coffee Republic Academy. We were hiring a lot of baristas at the time and really needed a dedicated training academy to teach them about the Coffee Republic way of making coffee drinks. We had heard about McDonalds University and had always dreamed of having one of our own.

To achieve this goal, yet again we had to bootstrap. We did not know anything about how to formally set up an Academy or creating a training manual, and nor did anyone we had hired. We could not afford to pay a professional to do it for us, so we had to work everything out for ourselves. But as you'll have realised by now, once you put your mind to it you can do almost anything.

In reality, opening the Academy proved easier than we expected it would be. We got all the equipment from the suppliers on loan and put the graphics Adrian had done for the Academy on the door. Bingo – the Coffee Republic Academy was born!

We never thought we could write a training manual and when later on we hired people who were familiar with professional training manuals we realised that our own efforts had been surprisingly good. Few of our employees had seen a training manual before – especially not one related to coffee – but once we put our minds to it, because we had no other choice, what we came up with was more than passably good.

Sahar was left in charge of this process and she put down on paper everything she thought was important about making the right coffee drink. With Eva's help, we produced such a good manual that it is still used at Coffee Republic to this day.

The third store, then, did make a real difference for us. Having Marco full time was a huge benefit because now there was someone other than us looking after the Coffee Republic business. It was a great feeling! We still managed to visit all three bars each morning and we remained very hands-on. It was still a baby.

The bootstrapping continued. Sahar was still signing the weekly barista pay cheques every Wednesday and it was her task to deliver them to the stores in her car. Many a time Marco had to chase Sahar for paycheques she would forget to deliver, but in the end the system worked, albeit not without a lot of pleading and chasing from those involved at the sharp end.

With the same structure still in place, we opened a tiny store on London Wall in March, another in June on the Strand, and in August yet another store on Fleet Street. All these stores did well. Each had a slow start but we were getting brand recognition and goodwill working on our side so our sales were on an upward curve from day one. We did some basic marketing, leafleting offices nearby and providing free samples outside the shops, and we were lucky in that the path was much smoother for us than it had been with South Molton Street. By this time, people knew about coffee bars so they were almost waiting for them to open. Our loyalty cards also helped.

On Fleet Street, we were the first new style coffee bar and the bankers and lawyers flocked through our doors in droves. It was a real joy for us to see. Neighbouring investment banks would order 14 coffee drinks at a time and there were always queues outside our door.

Still, every night the barista on closing rota would call our home answerphone and report the days till sales. "It's Thomas from London Wall: £600", "It's Tanya from Strand: £500", were familiar refrains and we still waited for the calls with eager anticipation and had bets on how each store would day every day between ourselves.

By the summer of 1997 we had six stores. The activity in our flat had intensified to such a level that we knew it was time to move into professional offices as home was no longer home; we had reached a breaking point. The lucky thing had been that home was a portered block of flats and we had the ground floor flat which coincidentally had the porter's desk right outside. Thus, courier delivery and pick up were all taken care of easily. However, the long suffering porters had ended up playing the role of Coffee Republic receptionists and they were probably the first to feel delighted that we were moving on to the next stage.

Our trips to Prontoprint in Earls Court had become so frequent that the staff there felt that Coffee Republic was their little start up as well as ours! We needed our own photocopier too as our fax machine was no longer an acceptable method of making reproductions at home. We also needed to hire office staff to help us and we couldn't really have them working from our home as well. We simply reached a point where we needed to up the ante and evolve into a professional business. You can't do that in your sitting room with a TV in the corner and armchairs all around you. And, when you try, not only do you lack a professional office but you also lose the use of your living room as a place to relax.

Six stores, a growing business, full time staff...our original resources, sufficient at the start, were strained and bursting at the seams.

Preparing for growth: the market
Even with six stores, market pressure was still such that further growth was demanded. The coffee boom was exploding further by the day and Seattle Coffee Company, on whom we had set our sights, had already opened 30 stores. There were also serious rumours at this time about the big US chains coming to London. Whitbread had just bought Costa Coffee. The press interest was still increasing with the Financial Times reporting that the "UK is poised for the same gourmet coffee shop phenomenon sweeping the US".

We needed to step up our expansion plans. We were doing well but we had to capitalise on what we had done so far. It was very clear to us that we were in a market where there was a vast gulf between big and small. We either had to grow aggressively and thrive, or to fade into nothing at all if we missed the boat.

We were not 'destinations.' We had to be on every corner; as we had said in our first business plan: "Customers will not walk more than two blocks to get to their nearest coffee bar."

With the conditions we'd described, six stores would amount to suicide if we didn't move on quickly so we embarked on the next stage of growth.

CHILDHOOD YEARS

Bobby started on the third business plan in the spring of 1997; this time the aim was to open another 35 stores over the next two years.

"Coffee Republic is a concept with tremendous growth prospects. Management believes the success of Starbucks and other startup coffee chains in the US and the inconsistent and inferior quality of the UK coffee market presents a ripe opportunity for a US-style specialty coffee concept tailored to the UK market."

To meet these ambitious targets, we would need about £4.5m. It's not easy raising that sort of sum. Although Bobby had an investment banking background in New York, he didn't really have any contacts in the City or access to that kind of fund raising.

As he was pondering what to do, he had another 'entrepreneurial gut instinct' moment. He remembered that Sahar's close friend from her university days, Clare, was the daughter of Jim Slater, the 1970s takeover guru. He had tremendous admiration for Slater, having read all the accounts of his deals in the 1970s with Sir James Goldsmith.

Bobby asked Sahar to arrange an appointment with Jim Slater. He had no idea what he wanted from him, rather he just had a hunch that the contact would be a productive one. Sahar was reluctant to arrange the meeting as she knew that Jim was very exact and challenging, and she was worried that with no specific thing to ask him, they might make fools of themselves. But Bobby persisted and Sahar gave in eventually.

The following week we were sitting in Jim Slater's London house in Kensington telling him all about our plans for our chain of 6 coffee bars. Jim was very kind to us in the way that parents are to friends of their children. When we left we did feel a little bit foolish as we had had nothing really concrete to ask him. So we put the meeting out of our minds.

The next day Bobby got a call on his mobile. "Bobby, it's Jim Slater. I have a proposition for you." Jim had a shell company listed on AIM. His idea was for Coffee Republic to reverse into this shell company, thereby allowing Coffee Republic to raise funds through the market for opening 14 stores. It was the perfect financial vehicle to allow Coffee Republic to expand.

After many interesting meetings and negotiations with Jim Slater the reversal finally happened on 19 September 1997. We ended up keeping 27% of the newly enlarged group.

It wasn't a great financial deal for us, but we needed to grow so we needed money and we very much thought our own financial gain was secondary to the benefits Coffee Republic could gain from the floatation. Now, thinking back on it, the success of Coffee Republic was all that mattered to us. In the back of our minds we took a long-term view and believed that if we made the business a success, we would benefit eventually.

Preparing for growth: the business

It was our new profile as a PLC that really kicked the baby into childhood in one fell swoop. By the end of September 1997, Coffee Republic was listed on AIM. The public company aspect immediately changed our profile and added new, far tighter restrictions than we had ever faced before.

We had a proper board of directors that we had to report to every two months in the course of a very formal board meeting. We had institutional shareholders and financial advisors. All of a sudden we had a host of new parties involved in Coffee Republic, each with their own opinions and agendas.

The great thing for both of us was that we were sitting back at the boardroom table, this time not as minions in a law firm or an investment bank but as clients. Our journey had come full circle – from the boardroom table to our kitchen table and back to the boardroom table again.

We hired a finance director as PLCs are required to do and this gave us another reason for moving into offices. We could hardly expect someone of this level to work from our home. We make this point because, although it may seem obvious, it shows just how each step on the road has repercussions that have to be faced as they happen.

It was a challenge finding economical office space in Central London. We believed that it was important for our head office to be near our stores, and these were all in the West End where prices are astronomical. We found great office space in Parson's Green and other areas, but we really didn't want to work so far away from the heart of things. Finally we had an amazing stroke of luck in that our surveyors had a floor of office space on Albermarle Street that they were stuck with and were more than happy to sublet to us at a very good rate as it was the fagend of a long-term lease. When we were doing our presentations for going public we will never forget the disapproving looks we got for choosing Mayfair offices. No one believed that we were paying such cheap rents.

Getting office space coincided with our need to expand the management team to prepare for our next round of business expansion. With a Finance Director in place, Marco and his by now small but growing accounting team moved in as well. We hired a Human Resources manager to handle all recruitment and training. Before that the store managers or the Operations Manager did the hiring and the training, but with our planned rate of growth we needed someone dedicated purely to that role. With new team members on board we had to define our own roles as well; Bobby became CEO and Sahar Marketing Director of Coffee Republic. We even hired a receptionist!

But despite this new PLC status and structure, the company was still entrepreneurial in character. Our new team members were all entrepreneurial in spirit. They weren't big company types to the extent that they fitted in to the flexible structure we had. It was as if we had a team of entrepreneurs and not just us. Each of us was a jack of all trades. Marco managed the office as well as being the bookeeper. Beth, our receptionist, helped with the marketing and took on a supportive role to our bar managers. This made the atmosphere in the office very special and it was during this period that we have perhaps our fondest memories of working in the business we'd founded.

The amazing thing about the Albemarle Street years was that everyone had the same passion that we did about Coffee Republic. We were all there to serve the increasing needs of this fast growing company. No one really cared about position or title. The only thing that mattered was Coffee Republic itself. And everyone managed to laugh a lot of the time, as well as to work incredibly hard.

This period was also very rewarding for all of us. In life cycle terms Coffee Republic was really taking its first independent steps, learning to talk and more. The entire team were devoted to the upbringing of this being, and shared in the joy of seeing it mature.

Growing...
In the year we went public, we opened 13 stores. We were getting access to better locations and so we were able to open in King's Road, Fulham Road, Notting Hill, Covent Garden, Cornhill, and generally all the places we had always dreamt of opening Coffee Republic shops. Our business was really becoming a part of London life!

We also saw a lot of dreams we had for the brand come to fruition. Having seen the 'sip'n'browse' concept in the US, we always wanted to open outlets in bookstores and we finally got a deal to put Coffee Republics in Waterstones – our first being in their Trafalgar Square shop.

The really difficult nut to crack had been Heathrow. Most people who start a chain dream of Heathrow. You have a captive audience and it's a great showpiece. We tried right from the beginning to get in and despite many meetings and a great deal of pleading we had no success. But once we had over 10 stores the authorities there started to give us the time of day.

We were eventually offered the domestic arrivals area. It wasn't ideal as we would have much preferred international departures, but we were so grateful that we took it.

In the years 1997 and 1998 we really set out to establish our brand as a lifestyle brand. We still didn't have big money to throw at it so we did what is referred to as 'guerrilla marketing'. Guerrilla marketing refers to merging your entrepreneurial spirit with the marketing message you send out to customers. It's really about bootstrapping again: you use every resource you have with all your gut instincts, faith and energy in tow so that two plus two equals five.

For example we couldn't afford to advertise, so our only solution to getting press attention was through PR. PR is a much more economical way to promote your brand. Whereas it costs over £15,000 to advertise on one page in a glossy, write-ups are free. Yet an editorial write-up has three times more credibility than an advert. In choosing a PR company to get our name out and about, we didn't want to go with consumer PR companies which conventionally represented 'boring' food brands. We positioned ourselves not as a utilitarian brand but as a lifestyle brand and so we made the unusual move of enlisting Aurelia PR, who specialised in sexy, high-fashion brands like Versace, Tag Heuer and Krug champagne. We were thus able to piggyback on the attention press normally give high-spending brands. Additionally, we used ourselves as marketing messages for Coffee Republic.

People are more interesting than products (how much can you write on coffee), so we used that to promote our business.

And we did build up a great deal of press coverage. Having a good consistent product helped; we won all taste tests, beating our competitors by miles. We made a poster showing the results and put it in our stores.

To make up for our lack of marketing expertise on other things, we went with our instincts and the only question we kept asking ourselves was 'as a customer would I like this?' or 'as a customer what would I love to read at my local coffee bar?'. The answers to the questions became the basis of our marketing campaigns.

Instead of looking at marketing as a whole project, we made it manageable by looking at every individual customer experience. Marketing for us lay in exploiting the opportunity provided by the 5-20 minutes each customer spent in our bar. We needed to make sure that they had a high-quality experience that enhanced their day. Through marketing, we set out to promote the idea that we were a business that delivered its promises on a consistent basis. If we could get this across to one customer at a time, then effective marketing would be able to meet a manageable goal.

Right from the beginning we spoke with one voice to the customer. And that voice, because it was genuine and we consistently delivered on what we said we would do, established a real and lasting dialogue. In effect, by being genuine and really believing in our message and the rapport with our customers, we made up for our lack of marketing expertise.

There was no rocket science behind building the Coffee Republic brand. It was a brand built from the heart. It had acquired a soul and with it, a unique voice. Customers believed our voice because we lived up to our word. Honesty is more valuable than any marketing gimmick that money can buy. It is the foundation for a genuine dialogue with the customer.

We kept trying new drinks and food ideas every day in Albermarle Street so the business was constantly innovative. We called the tiny office kitchen (which to be honest was more of a cupboard than anything else) the 'R&D department'. Everyone would get involved and give their opinion on new products. The great thing about this sort of atmosphere was that new ideas would get implemented very quickly; there was no red tape or 'why?' Everything was 'why not?' instead.

Beth, our receptionist, started working closely with Sahar on marketing and she soon became the full-time marketing assistant so we hired another receptionist. For the summer, we wanted the ice blended drinks we had seen in the USA to go on sale (these are now called our 'FREEZERS') but since we couldn't find a supplier (they still didn't exist for some things) we made them from scratch from a recipe Sahar found on the Internet and tweaked it until it tasted right. The result wasn't great and it was a nightmare to prepare but we tried it anyway and the customers loved it because it was the best you could get at the time.

Seeing a lot of kids coming in in the morning with their parents to our bars in residential areas, we invented the BabyCap, which was a fake cappuccino (hot chocolate with foam) in a tiny cup. We even got press coverage for this!

Since our customers were coming in on a daily basis by this time, we wanted to offer them excitement and seasonal changes so we had special drinks made up for every special time of year: Love Latte for Valentines Day, the Green Halloween Latte, The Yuletide Latte, the Cookiecinno Freezer, and more. We even had a World Cup Latte during the 1998 World Cup. Our unofficial motto was "During the holidays, corniness prevails." Since we couldn't use sophisticated marketing tactics, we thought sheer corniness would grab the attention of customers and press alike.

Our voice had a sense of humour about it and we didn't mind making fools of ourselves. We think that our customers found this endearing. The great thing was that as we were thinking of everything as customers ourselves, it made the thinking easier and the results better. For a while we even had a 'pet store' scheme. Each employee chose a pet store that they would quality control on a weekly basis.

By this point in time suppliers were lining up to provide new types of coffee bar 'gourmet products' to the market, so every day we were inundated with sample cakes, chocolate, doughnuts and more. Nobody at Coffee Republic ever had to go out and buy lunch or any food of any kind: there was always a full basket in reception.

As far as our internal marketing went, we now had hundreds of employees and communicating our entrepreneurial spirit to them was a challenge. Inspired by retail entrepreneur Julian Richer's book, we implemented the 'tell Bobby' programme, which incentivised employees working in stores around the country to send suggestions to Bobby. The best one each week was rewarded with a small cheque.

Sahar, in an 'entrepreneurial gut-instinct moment' thought we should have a company newsletter to keep everyone who worked at Coffee Republic in our faraway outposts up to date with what was going on. She had no idea how to start one but remembered a great one at her law firm and so she personally typed the first copy of CR News. To make it juicy we had a celeb-spotting column reporting the celebrities visiting our stores. These are things that, with a little imagination and a dose of energy, anyone can do instantly.

ADOLESCENT YEARS

Preparing for growth: the market

If you think it sounds like we were growing quickly, the market was moving even faster. By end of summer 1998 what we had dreaded from the beginning finally happened. Starbucks, the US giant, bought our competitor, the Seattle Coffee Company. Starbucks already had 1000 stores in the US, it was a billion dollar company and it had a huge marketing force. They spent millions on advertising whilst we were spending almost nothing. They had an R&D department; we had our cupboard. They had a marketing budget in the millions whilst ours lay in the four figures. They had world marketing experts; we simply had our own gut instincts.

Starbucks opened their first UK store on the King's Road with a huge fanfare. We knew from the USA that their arrival in new territories severely threatened the already established brands there and few of them survived after Starbuck's marketing might took root. We were determined not to let this happen to Coffee Republic. To our advantage, we were the first mover in the market and had gained brand loyalty. Customers liked us and so most of them remained loyal. All we needed to do was to keep our standards and consistency high and open more stores.

In our world things change very quickly. We moved into our head office in November 1997 and by the end of 1998 we had doubled in size. We had been adding specialist layers of people to do all the jobs we did ourselves when we were smaller. For example, Bobby used to go around looking for sites and with us opening a store every fortnight that year, 'pavement pounding' was too time consuming for a CEO so we hired a property manager to work with surveyors and help find good sites and solve this problem. For store designs and shop fitting we hired a project manager. We moved our Academy to a larger space in the basement of our Garrick Street bar and hired a dedicated training manager.

Our accounts department grew especially fast. Being a cash business this was inevitable. In the end, we had to send Marco and his team back to Queensway as there was no longer space for them at head office.

We don't remember exactly when but at some point in autumn of 1998 we realised that we had to move to the next stage. With the increasing pressures of growth, Coffee Republic had to grow up as well as grow.

Growing up...

As any company grows the essential bond it has at first is harder and harder to maintain. However great a team is, success brings with it volumes and numbers that are just too big to deal with without a proper structure. It's true that without passion and vision a business has no soul, but passion and vision alone aren't enough to sustain a company through such a boom. Processes, systems, discipline and professionalism are needed too, and inevitably this became the case for Coffee Republic.

At the end of 1998 we numbered 20 stores. We could no longer visit them all so personal quality control didn't work any more and we couldn't possibly know each and every one of our employees. There was a danger that if we didn't do something, lack of structure would affect the consistency of what we offered to our customers.

Textbook business theory says that as the business gets bigger, it needs to invest in an organisational 'culture' as a substitute for the influence of personalities of the founders. Small organisations don't have 'cultures'. Instead they have personalities and usually the personality they assume is that of the founder. As the business grows, the founder's personality has less influence. This is a matter of simple mathematics of course; the light from the personality of the founder finds it difficult to penetrate as far as those outer orbits of the larger organisation.

The need for a culture became a serious issue for us. As well as our creative, flexible, informal and personality-based qualities on which Coffee Republic had been founded, we also recognised the need for a drier process based on implementing the systems and controls necessary to ensure the business continued to run effectively. If we failed to put these in place, we wouldn't be able to cope with the pressures of growth. It was no longer a good thing that everyone did everything. Our informality – precisely what had brought us to life – ultimately came to endanger the quality and consistency of our product. We needed systems in place that didn't rely on goodwill alone.

With the market heating up and the arrival of Starbucks we had to ensure that all our stores were delivering the Coffee Republic experience perfectly and consistently every minute of the day. The only way to do that was through employees: by attracting, training and motivating the best. Coffee Republic needed to be a place where everyone wanted to work. We needed a culture that could then have a life and force of its own, quite separate from its founders, and built from the ground up.

At the time we had read in a catering magazine about a well respected figure who was looking to move on. His team-building techniques were legendary in the business. He was a true people person and exactly what we needed. He could create the culture for us, and we pursued him vigorously.

He joined us as MD in January 1999. His arrival heralded the growth of Coffee Republic out of childhood.

Preparing for growth: the Business
Our new MD joined us with a view to bringing in a professional management culture to sustain us through very rapid growth. We had planned 30 bars per year. The idea was for him to take the child into adulthood. But as with our life cycle analogy earlier, you don't go from childhood to adulthood unless you pass through the turbulent years of adolescence.

Since he was such a people person, he brought with him a team all of whom had worked with him before and swore by his methods. Soon, everyone wanted to work for Coffee Republic. They came from far and away, and everyone he had worked with before at TGI and Pret having heard about our exciting developments wanted to join up. We almost immediately had a management culture.

Bobby remained CEO and dealt with all things financial, including raising further funds for expansion. Sahar remained Marketing Director with a marketing assistant and a newly hired buying manager working in her department.

Life in hyper-growth business, though, is never straightforward and just when everything seemed to be settling into place, suddenly everything changed once again!

It was very exciting having high calibre, highly-trained employees of a quality we had not been able to attract before, but overnight there seemed to be so many of them. The new people practically stampeded in and immediately controls and systems and training manuals were put into place and formal communication lines established, but it seemed as though barriers were being put up around each person's desk. There were clear delineations of roles and responsibilities, with almost no flexibility between them. Not, in other words, the 'old' Coffee Republic at all.

We were about to become big (if we weren't big already) and so Coffee Republic became an adolescent adjusting to adulthood and trying to abandon its childhood qualities overnight. The change proved too much for many of our original team who were all becoming disenchanted, as their work no longer involved the same feeling they had loved so much at the start. Coffee Republic wasn't the same company. Now it was 'big business'.

Eventually, all of the original team saw the end of the road and we lost them in the course of a few months. We found this very sad, especially Marco's departure in the spring of 2000 which was very hard for us to take on a personal level. The signals that a phase in the life of Coffee Republic was ending were clear and many tears were shed at Marco's leaving party.

Growing Pains - Culture clash
Normally, the person that this change hits hardest is the entrepreneur. For Sahar, who had always embodied the entrepreneur within the organisation, the evolution of styles was felt very strongly and she found it difficult to swallow. Suddenly she was a manager and not a dreamer and implementer. She became

head of a Marketing Department with corporate constraints and formal lines of reporting. Every morning there were management meetings, reviews, performance management systems in place, and more. It was no longer trying out new products in the kitchen and being open to every new suggestion. There were more 'it's impossible' comments than times when she heard 'why not?' The dreaming phase was over.

There is a famous saying that Henry Ford used when he tried to get his assembly line working faster though all the workers who had worked on it for years were telling him how things were moving as quickly as they could. Ford said "Then go get me some 25 year olds who don't know it can't be done."

Having a highly experienced team is a double-edged sword. While an entrepreneurial company lives its life out of the box, a mature organisation exists in its box. Conventional wisdom becomes a prevailing philosophy. Having experienced people running the show put Coffee Republic into a box, and with so many rules and ways of doing things the company was no longer open to trying new things. There were always millions of reasons why nothing new could be done. (Remember the importance of being clueless?)

We weren't the first and will not be the last entrepreneurs to feel the clash of cultures. It's an inevitable result of growth and the need for maintaining the fine and delicate balance between between being professionals and being entrepreneurs.

Another result we saw from our newly professional structure is that the business was now much more internally focused. More importance was attached to what was happening internally than externally in the world of the Coffee Republic customer. It was very bizarre seeing that change of priorities happen. This change of focus from external to internal is a very typical symptom of a maturing business and a typical grievance of most entrepreneurs.

There were a great many healthy (and heated) debates between us, the founders, and our management team. Brand values versus profit! A great example of this was on the importance of the coffee blend. For Sahar, changing the coffee blend was an encroachment of the DNA and she fought for it. There were thereafter many similar battles on other issues: automatic machines, selling Coca Cola, retaining loyalty cards, changing music away from classical and opera, and more. In every case Sahar the entrepreneur withstood change whilst the new MD fought avidly for it.

Some he did win. We removed our very popular loyalty cards which entitled the customer to a tenth drink free. The MD thought they opened the way for abuse. It was fine on a small scale but with 25 plus stores it wasn't practical to control the freebies offered. 'Free' was not the right button to have on the till of a multi-bar organisation. And he was right. It would have been nice to keep the scheme but it wasn't practical anymore.

We also lost the classical music that Sahar thought integral to CR. But listening to Jazz FM now, its not really so bad! Perhaps change was the right thing there, too.

But despite the clashes with Sahar in her role of entrepreneur, the new team did a fabulous job. In 1999 and 2000 Coffee Republic opened almost 50 stores. That rate of growth puts serious pressures on a business but the new team was strong and professional enough to sustain it.

The millennium brought great heights for Coffee Republic. We were named in a market report in the Financial Times as one of five brands representing New Britain. We did a great promotion with Tate Modern when they were opening in May 2000 and chose us as their launch partner. It was a great honour for us to be chosen and it was great team building to be involved in such a momentous monument in London.

We were opening new branches at extraordinarily quick rates, but we had a dedicated bar-opening team to do the job, full of energy and enthusiasm and turning each new business into a Coffee Republic the customer recognised almost from the first minute. The times may have been different than they were at first, but they were still very exciting.

We were always invited to the 'graduation ceremony' that would happen before each store opening, to celebrate completion of training a new team of baristas. It was wonderful and slightly melancholy at the same time, just coming in as guests to these perfect new bars which we really had no hands-on part in opening. It must be the way parents feel going to an adult child's graduation. You are proud of what you've produced but slightly in awe of this new autonomous person in front of you. One that really no longer needs you to survive.

The real change came when our MD declared that we had to move out of Albemarle Street, as we were too big for it. We needed to have the whole company under the same roof and we still had accounts in Queensway and human resources in Garrick Street.

For us, that was really the moment when we finally realised that Coffee Republic no longer needed us. The move would be the last step of the journey into adulthood for our business. We felt our entrepreneurial stage was over and therefore we were no longer pivotal to the company. We had survived the spotty teenage years and maintained the DNA intact. The time had come to let go.

EPILOGUE:

To a certain extent, after we had moved into new offices at London Bridge, we felt much less at ease. We were less happy working for what was now a professionally managed business with all the processes and systems and hierarchies that goes with it. Coffee Republic had reached adulthood, and where its founders were concerned, their role had irretrievably changed. We had built the sort of business that we wanted to get away from in the first place. The wheel had turned full circle.

A common phenomenon of the maturity of the business is the departure of the founders. The legends of business growth always warn against founders who stay too long and buck the unspoken rule that at some point the time comes for the founder to exit. Ignore this rule and you become like an 'over-controlling parent stunting the growth of your offspring'. There is the long-held belief that entrepreneurs never make good managers.

We always knew our time eventually had to come. That point came for us in April 2001.

Coffee Republic was a fully independent adult, strong, with a soul and the right values, and we realised that it should go out on its own with its new team.

It was a very sad realisation for us. They say that entrepreneurs equate leaving the company they founded with the emotions and feelings of bereavement. It's true. The separation was enormously painful for us.

Sahar was on a flight back from the US the day the Financial Times broke the news of her and Bobby's stepping down from their management roles at Coffee Republic. She found a copy of the FT in the British Airways lounge and burst into uncontrollable tears. The other passengers were aghast at what was quite so painful and tragic in a business newspaper that it might warrant such a burst of emotion.

But they will never know. Even if they knew, they wouldn't understand.

Because they were never entrepreneurs...

Our Entrepreneurial Rolodex

THE BEST 'HOW TO' BOOKS

Lloyds TSB Small Business Guide by Sara Williams
The Complete Small Business Guide by Colin Barrow

For any potential entrepreneurs these should be your bibles!

MARKET RESEARCH

The following institution is really invaluable for all sorts of info.
Definitely make it your first port of call

City Business Library
1 Brewers Hall Garden
London EC2V 5BX
Tel: 0207 332 1812
www.cityoflondon.gov.uk

If you are short of time for desk research (or too far away) then you can call their
fee based research service:
Business Information Focus
Tel: 0207 600 1461

BUSINESS PLAN

There are a lot of books on writing business plans. The Lloyds
Small Business Guide has a great chapter on business plans.

Business Plan Services
www.bizplans.co.uk
Helps you with all aspects of business planning and writing a business plan (for a fee)

RAISING MONEY

For bank loans, high street banks have small business divisions. Your best bet is to try them all.

For information on Government loans/grants and free advice on starting up:
Business Link
Tel: 0845 6009006
www.businesslink.org

The Prince's Trust
www.princes-trust.org.uk
The Business Programme provides low interest loans, grants and mentors for 18-30 year olds who have a good business idea but can't get funding.

Business Angels Network
www.VCR1978.com
They match entrepreneurs to angel investors

FORMING A LTD COMPANY AND REGISTERING THE NAME:

Companies house
www.companieshouse.gov.uk

To register your 'aha!' name/logo as a trademark or if you want to check if anyone else has already registered it as a trademark search the Patent Office web site
www.patent.gov.uk

Do this all as quickly as possible before someone else beats you to it!

SUPPORT NETWORKS

BusyGirl.com
Europe's leading corporate and entrepreneurial women's network

INDEX

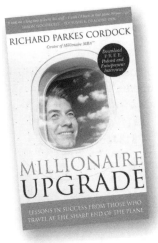